Applications of Artificial Intelligence and Machine Learning

SANTOSH REDDY ADDULA
R. DURGA MEENA
E.GEETHA RANI
D. ANUSHA

NOTION PRESS

NOTION PRESS

India. Singapore. Malaysia.

ISBN 000-0-00473-85-5

Contents

Preface

Though still relatively new, the idea of machine learning and its vast potential for use are not widely known among students. In order to make machine learning ideas easy for techies, college students, and young managers to understand, we felt it would be a good idea to write this book especially for them. They had to comprehend the ideas underlying the machine learning software programs in addition to using them. Machine learning is finding more and more applications every day. Machine learning is finding applications in every aspect of life, from helping doctors diagnose patients to forecasting the real estate market, recommending products to consumers, and optimising energy use to support Green Earth initiatives.

1. Introduction to the Era of Artificial Intelligence and Machine Learning

The simulation of human intelligence in robots that are designed to think and behave like people is known as artificial intelligence, or AI. It entails the creation of computer programs and algorithms that are capable of carrying out operations like speech recognition, visual perception, decision-making, and language translation that normally demand for human intellect. Artificial intelligence (AI) has a broad range of applications, from self-driving cars to virtual personal assistants, and it has the potential to transform many sectors.

Let's first discuss the definition of intelligence before moving on to the notion of artificial intelligence. The capacity to learn and solve issues is intelligence. Webster's Dictionary provided this definition. "To make computers intelligent so they can act intelligently!" is the most typical response that one anticipates, but to what extent? How is intelligence measured? As perceptive as people. Computers would be deemed "intelligent" if they could in some way solve problems in the real world by learning from their mistakes and growing independently.

As a result, AI systems are more flexible, more generic, and capable of "thinking," as opposed to being particular. We all know that intelligence is the capacity to learn and use knowledge.

Experience imparts information, which is known as knowledge. Knowledge acquired through exposure (training) is referred to as experience. In summary, artificial intelligence can be defined as a "replica of something natural (i.e., humans) 'WHO' is capable of acquiring and applying the information it has gained through exposure."

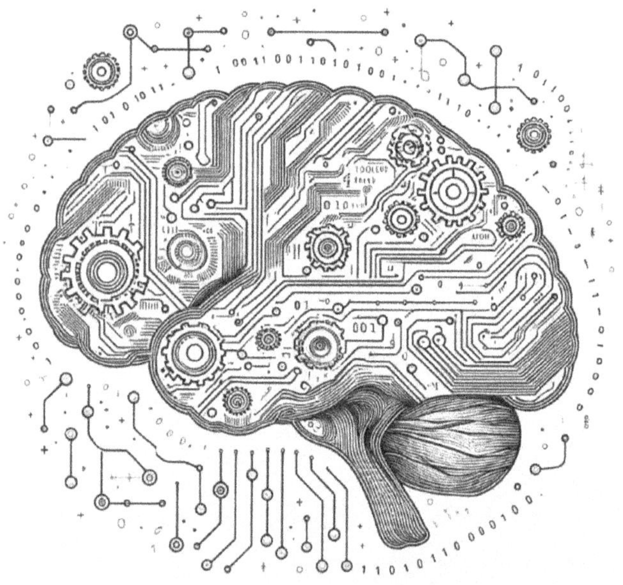

Figure.1.1 Artificial Intelligence

Artificial Intelligence (AI) uses a wide range of tools, such as probability and economics-based techniques, logic, and variations of search and mathematical optimization. AI draws from a wide range of disciplines, including artificial psychology, neuroscience, computer science, mathematics, psychology, languages, and philosophy. Artificial intelligence is primarily concerned with comprehending human performance and behavior.

Applications of Artificial Intelligence and Machine Learning
By building computers with human-like intelligence and capacities, this can be accomplished. This covers robotics, facial analysis, and natural language processing. The military, healthcare, and computer industries are where artificial intelligence is now being used most; however, it is anticipated that these industries will soon begin to use AI in their daily operations.

Many theories predict that computers will eventually become more intelligent than people because they will be able to learn more quickly, absorb information more efficiently, and make judgments more quickly. But there are still a lot of obstacles to overcome before artificial intelligence can truly be considered fully developed. For instance, computers struggle with physical activities like operating heavy machinery or driving cars, and they perform poorly in unsafe or chilly conditions. Nevertheless, artificial intelligence has a lot of fascinating things in store.

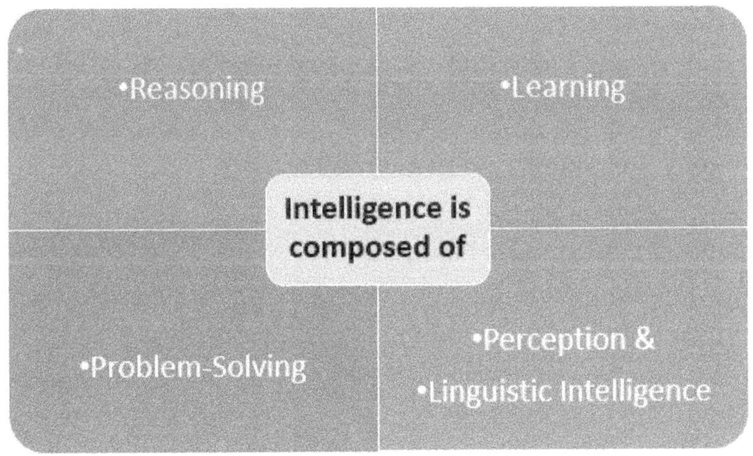

Figure. 1.2 Intelligence Composition

An approach to data analysis called machine learning automates the process of creating analytical models. This area of artificial intelligence is predicated on the notion that machines are capable of learning from data, spotting patterns, and making judgments with little help from humans.

Do you receive recommendations for movies you should watch next on Netflix and Amazon Prime automatically? Or perhaps you see People You Might Know options on LinkedIn or Facebook? You may also use your phones' Siri, Alexa, and other features. All of that is machine learning! This is a technology that is gaining increasing traction. It's likely that practically all of the technology in your environment uses machine learning!

Moreover, the idea is scarcely novel. The ability of robots to learn on their own without extensive human programming has always captivated researchers. Nevertheless, with the advent of big data in the present era, this has gotten considerably simpler to accomplish. Much more precise Machine Learning algorithms that work in the technical sector can be made using large data sets. Therefore, even though machine learning has been around for a while, it is currently a buzzword in the field.

However, are you still unsure about what machine learning actually is? Which are its multiple varieties, and which are the distinct Machine Learning algorithms? Find the answers to all of your questions by reading on!

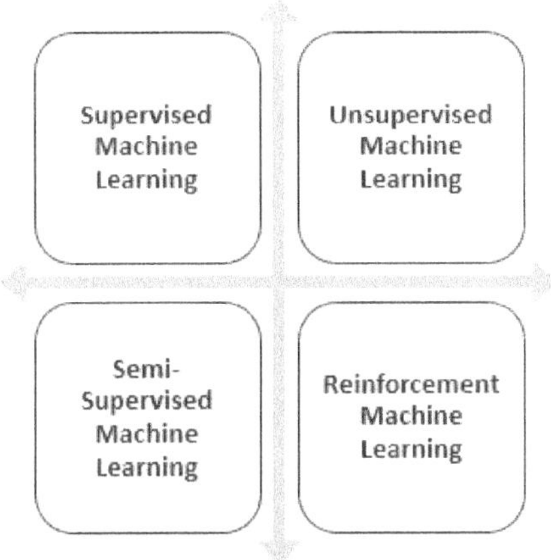

Figure. 1.3 Various Type of Machine Learning

As the name suggests, machine learning is the process of computers learning on their own without explicit programming or human assistance. The first step in the machine learning process is to give the machines high-quality data. After that, the machines are trained by creating different machine learning models with the data and various algorithms.

The kind of task we are aiming to automate and the type of data we have will determine which algorithms we choose. The formal definition of machine learning is as follows: if an algorithm's performance at tasks in T, as determined by P, improves with experience E, then the algorithm learns from experience E with regard to some sort of task T and performance metric P.

Take chess, for instance, where a machine learning algorithm is employed. Then, the task T is to play chess with several players, the experience E is to play numerous games of chess, and the performance measure P is the likelihood that the algorithm will win.

Figure. 1.4 Things of Machine Learning

1.1. Key difference between AI and ML

While there are some similarities between machine learning and artificial intelligence, there are also some differences. The broad goal of artificial intelligence is to produce intelligence that is similar to that of humans. Artificial intelligence is a broad term that refers to the process of giving robots reasoning and critical thinking abilities similar to those of humans. Conversely, machine learning is a branch of artificial intelligence that focuses on building machines that can learn from data on their own. Because machine learning is specialized rather than generic, it enables a machine to use data to predict outcomes or make decisions about a particular issue. AI-powered machine learning continuously learns from data, rule-based systems rely on predetermined

Applications of Artificial Intelligence and Machine Learning business rules. Although rule-based systems are straightforward and economical, they are not flexible and have bias and ambiguity issues. Machine learning systems are more dynamic, flexible, and capable of managing challenging circumstances.

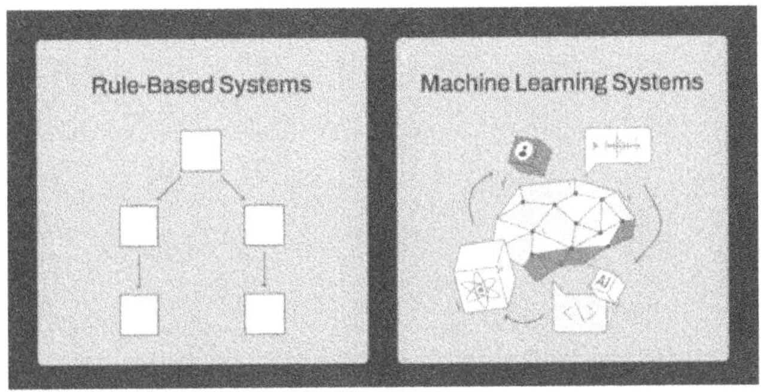

Figure. 1.5 Rule based AI verses Machine Learning Systems

To create AI models for particular applications, artificial intelligence (AI) engineers work on a wider range of tasks that encompass different types of machine intelligence, such as neural networks. On the other hand, machine learning (ML) engineers concentrate increasingly on ML models and algorithms that have the ability to self-correct in order to learn from and forecast vast amounts of data more accurately.

The term artificial intelligence (AI) refers to a variety of methods and approaches that can be used to give robots more human-like characteristics. Robotic vacuum cleaners, self-driving automobiles, and smart assistants like Alexa are all examples of artificial intelligence (AI). Among the various subfields of artificial intelligence (AI) is machine learning (ML). The science of machine learning (ML) creates statistical models and algorithms that computer systems can utilize to carry out complicated tasks without explicit guidance. Instead, the systems rely on inference and patterns. Machine learning algorithms are used by computer systems to analyze vast amounts of historical data and spot trends in the data. Even though AI encompasses machine learning, not all AI endeavors involve machine learning.

One subset of artificial intelligence (AI) is machine learning (ML). Compared to AI, ML is more focused and has a smaller reach. A number of techniques and technologies used in AI are outside the purview of machine learning. These are the main distinctions between the two.

Goals

- Any AI system aims to make a machine capable of effectively completing a difficult human task. These kinds of tasks could entail learning, solving puzzles, and identifying patterns.
- However, machine learning (ML) aims to examine massive amounts of data by means of a machine. The device will find patterns in the data and generate a result by using statistical models. There is a corresponding degree of confidence or probability of correctness for the result.

Techniques

Artificial intelligence (AI) uses a range of techniques to address a wide range of issues. Neural networks, genetic algorithms, deep learning, search algorithms, rule-based systems, and machine learning itself are some of these techniques. Supervised and unsupervised learning are the two main categories into which

Applications of Artificial Intelligence and Machine Learning
machine learning techniques fall. ML algorithms under
supervision are trained to solve problems using input and output
data values labeled. Unsupervised learning is a more experimental
approach that looks for patterns that are hidden in unlabeled data.

Executions

Typically, developing an ML solution entails two steps: Choose
and get ready for a training dataset. Select a pre-existing machine
learning model or method, like decision trees or linear regression.

Important data features are chosen by data scientists and included
to the model during training. They regularly check for errors and
add current data to the dataset to make it better. The variety and
quality of the data enhance the ML model's accuracy. Since
creating an AI product is usually a more difficult process, many
people opt to accomplish their objectives by using prebuilt AI
solutions. Usually, the result of years of research, these AI
solutions are now made available for integration with goods and
services by developers via APIs.

Conditions

- A few hundred data points in a dataset are needed for
  training ML solutions, in addition to the processing
  capacity to operate them. You may need a single server
  instance or a small server cluster, depending on your use
  case and application.
- The infrastructure needed for other intelligent systems
  may differ depending on the goal you wish to achieve and
  the computational analytical approach you use. In high-

computing use cases, thousands of machines must cooperate to do intricate tasks.

- It's crucial to remember that prebuilt ML and AI functions are accessible. With APIs, you may include them into your program without requiring any more resources.

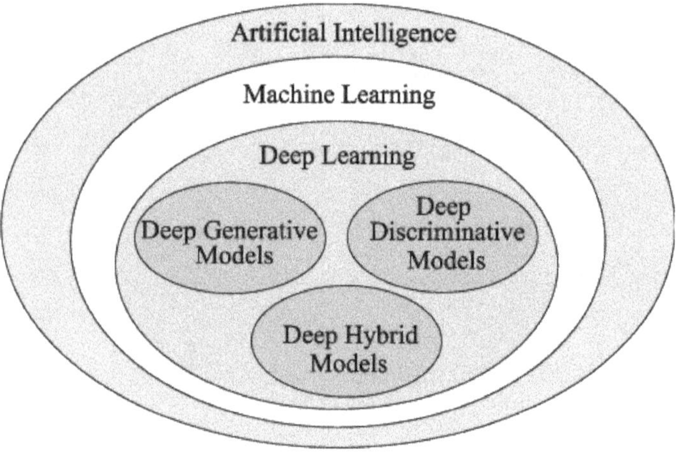

Figure. 1.6 Similarities between AI and Machine Learning

Machine learning is the process of teaching a machine to maximize a performance criterion by utilizing sample data or historical information. Our model is specified up to a point, and learning is the process of running a computer program to maximize the model's parameters based on training data or prior knowledge. The model might be descriptive to learn from data or predictive to make predictions about the future.

Building computer programs that automatically get better with experience is the focus of the branch of study known as machine learning. Within the science of artificial intelligence, machine

Applications of Artificial Intelligence and Machine Learning

learning focuses on creating statistical models and algorithms that allow computers to become more proficient at tasks over time. Without explicit guidance, these models and algorithms are made to learn from data and make predictions or judgments. Machine learning comes in a variety of forms, such as reinforcement learning, unsupervised learning, and supervised learning. A model is trained on labelled data in supervised learning, whereas an unsupervised model is trained on unlabelled data. Using trial and error, a model is trained in reinforcement learning. Natural language processing, recommender systems, and picture and speech recognition are just a few of the many uses for machine learning.

1.2 Need for AI and ML in Industries

Healthcare

AI & ML improving diagnosis precision, customizing treatment regimens, and streamlining hospital operations, AI and ML are transforming the healthcare industry. To help with early illness identification, medication development, and patient care, these technologies evaluate genetic data, medical imaging, and electronic health information.

Analysis of Medical Imaging:

Medical imaging, including MRIs, CT scans, and X-rays, may be analyzed by AI and ML algorithms to help with diagnosis, early illness identification, and treatment planning. With the use of these technologies, medical personnel may diagnose patients quickly and accurately by identifying malformations, cancers, and other abnormalities with great precision.

Using Risk Stratification and Predictive Analytics

In order to forecast illness risk, course, and patient outcomes, AI and ML models may evaluate patient data, including genetic information, lifestyle variables, and electronic health records (EHRs). These predictive analytics technologies assist medical professionals in identifying patients at high risk, acting quickly, and customizing treatment regimens to meet each patient's needs.

Drug Development and Discovery

Through the analysis of large datasets, identification of promising drug candidates, and prediction of their safety and effectiveness profiles, AI and ML are speeding up the drug discovery process. With the use of these technologies, researchers may expedite the drug development process, save expenses, and introduce novel medicines to patients sooner.

Individualized Medical Care

Through evaluating patient data to find the best treatments based on genetic composition, illness features, and therapy responses, AI and ML offer individualized treatment methods. With the use of these technologies, medical professionals may better target therapies, reduce side effects, and enhance patient outcomes.

Systems for Clinical Decision Support

Clinical decision support systems (CDSS) with AI capabilities offer physicians advice and suggestions in real time, based on patient data, medical literature, and industry best practices. By supporting diagnosis, treatment planning, and drug

Applications of Artificial Intelligence and Machine Learning administration, these tools improve professional judgment and patient safety.

Telemedicine and remote monitoring

Wearable technology and Internet of Things sensors allow for the remote monitoring of patients' vital signs, symptoms, and health measures thanks to AI and ML technologies. These technologies make it easier to obtain healthcare services, especially in underserved or rural places, and permit telemedicine consultations as well as early intervention for chronic disorders.

Optimizing Healthcare Operations

In evaluating operational data, patient flow, and resource use, AI and ML algorithms optimize hospital operations to increase productivity, decrease wait times, and improve patient happiness. These technologies aid healthcare institutions in optimizing capacity planning, streamlining operations, and wisely allocating resources.

Monitoring the Revenue Cycle and Fraud

Healthcare organizations employ AI and ML to identify fraud, inaccuracies in billing, and infractions of insurance policies and revenue cycle management regulations. With the purpose of preventing fraud, minimizing financial losses, and guaranteeing regulatory compliance, these tools evaluate claims data, spot abnormalities, and highlight questionable trends.

Clinical Trials and Medical Research

Through the analysis of patient data, genetic information, and biological literature, AI and ML enhance medical research and clinical trials by revealing novel insights, biomarkers, and treatment targets. These technologies increase trial enrolment and recruitment, speed up the development of new therapies, and improve the effectiveness of clinical trial procedures.

Patient Involvement and Modification of Behaviour

Through behaviour modification, progress tracking, and tailored health recommendations, AI and ML technologies include people in their healthcare journey. By utilizing patient-generated data, social determinants of health, and behavioural science concepts, these devices enable people to take charge of their health and make educated decisions.

Figure. 1.7 Need for AI and ML in Industries

Finance

Applications of Artificial Intelligence and Machine Learning Algorithmic trading, credit scoring, risk management, and fraud detection are among the financial services that employ AI and ML algorithms. By identifying patterns and trends in the massive volumes of financial data they examine, these technologies assist institutions in risk mitigation and decision-making.

Fraud Detection and Prevention

Algorithms powered by AI and ML are used to identify fraudulent activity in financial transactions, such as money laundering, credit card fraud, and identity theft. These solutions save financial losses and safeguard clients by analysing transaction data, user behaviour patterns, and past fraud instances to spot abnormalities and flag questionable activity in real time.

Algorithmic Trading and Forecasting the Market

For the purpose of spotting lucrative trading opportunities and forecasting market trends, AI and ML models examine market data, news sentiment, and trade patterns. Financial institutions can make data-driven investment decisions and maximize portfolio performance thanks to these technologies, which also support quantitative analysis, risk management, and algorithmic trading methods.

Risk assessment and credit scoring

AI and ML algorithms use borrower profiles, financial histories, and economic factors to anticipate default risk, analyze loan applications, and assess creditworthiness. By automating credit decisions, enhancing the precision of risk assessments, and providing customized lending solutions to clients, these technologies help lenders increase loan availability while lowering default rates.

Relationship Management for Customers

AI-driven CRM systems evaluate consumer information, interactions, and preferences to enhance customer engagement, tailor advertising campaigns, and make financial product recommendations. With the use of these technologies, financial institutions may target particular demographics, segment their clientele, and provide individualized services that cater to their requirements and preferences.

Trading and Portfolio Management on Autopilot

Algorithms using AI and ML may automate trading, rebalance investment portfolios, and improve asset allocation techniques by taking into account risk tolerance, market circumstances, and investment objectives. These innovations optimize profits for investors, asset managers, and hedge funds while improving trade efficiency and lowering human error.

Regulatory Reporting and Compliance

Financial institutions may monitor regulatory developments, verify adherence to industry standards and best practices, and comply with regulatory obligations with the use of AI and ML technology. To reduce compliance risks, avert fines, and uphold regulatory compliance, these systems evaluate transaction data, identify compliance infractions, and provide regulatory reports.

Market Monitoring and Risk Control

Applications of Artificial Intelligence and Machine Learning Algorithms using AI and ML keep an eye on market activity, spot market manipulation, and evaluate systemic risks to the stability of the financial system. To detect new threats, put risk mitigation plans into place, and prevent disruptions to the financial markets, these systems examine trade data, market volatility, and macroeconomic factors.

Comparative Study and Financial Analysis

Quantitative analysts and financial modelers may create prediction models, test trading strategies, and evaluate investment possibilities with the use of AI and ML approaches. These technologies estimate market risks, project asset values, and improve investment strategies by utilizing historical data, statistical techniques, and machine learning algorithms.

Customer Assistance and Support

Chatbots, virtual assistants, and speech recognition software driven by AI offer real-time problem solving, tailored customer care, and inquiry responses. In the financial sector, these technologies boost customer happiness, lower costs, and increase the effectiveness of customer service—all of which contribute to a better overall customer experience.

Fraud Prevention and Cybersecurity

Technologies like AI and ML strengthen cybersecurity defenses, identify cybersecurity threats, and stop financial system data breaches. These systems manage critical financial data and defend against cyberattacks by analyzing network traffic, spotting suspicious activity, and reacting quickly to security problems.

Retail establishment

Through optimizing pricing strategies, enhancing customer experiences, and boosting supply chain efficiency, AI and ML are indispensable in the retail industry. These technologies facilitate the operation of inventory management solutions, demand forecasting models, and recommendation systems, which in turn allow retailers to streamline operations and personalize their offerings.

Customized Promotion

In analyzing consumer data to find trends and preferences, AI and ML algorithms help merchants create tailored marketing strategies. This might include personalized messaging, product suggestions, and targeted promotions, which can boost conversion rates and foster greater client loyalty.

Forecasting Demand

For the purpose of optimizing inventory management, merchants may benefit from demand forecasting models driven by artificial intelligence. These algorithms analyze historical sales data, changes in the market, and external variables such as weather and economic indicators. This guarantees that the appropriate items are available at the appropriate time, lowers the likelihood of stockouts, and saves the expenses associated with excess inventory.

Optimization of the Inventory

Applications of Artificial Intelligence and Machine Learning Inventory levels may be optimized with the use of machine learning algorithms by estimating demand for particular goods, determining which items are moving slowly, and finding any irregularities in stock levels. In this way, businesses are able to keep their inventory levels at ideal levels, so lowering their carrying costs while simultaneously satisfying client demand.

Adjustable Prices

Using artificial intelligence, dynamic pricing algorithms make adjustments to prices in real time depending on a variety of criteria, including consumer behaviour, demand, and the pricing of competitors. This makes it possible for merchants to optimize revenue by simultaneously retaining profitability and pricing items in a competitive manner.

Automating the Customer Service Process

Chat bots and virtual assistants that are driven by artificial intelligence are able to answer client questions, offering product suggestions, and providing assistance with order tracking. This improves the customer support experience while simultaneously cutting operating expenses.

Prevention of Losses

The video from security cameras is analyzed by machine learning algorithms in order to discover potentially fraudulent or theft-related incidents and suspicious conduct. The proactive prevention of losses and the enhancement of security inside retail establishments are both facilitated by this.

Management of the Supply Chain

Using artificial intelligence and machine learning, supply chain operations may be optimized by forecasting the lead times of suppliers, locating transportation bottlenecks, and optimizing route schedules. Because of this, operational efficiency is increased, expenses are decreased, and interruptions in the supply chain are reduced to a minimum.

Image recognition and visual search capabilities

Customers are able to search for items using photos thanks to visual search technology that is driven by artificial intelligence. This improves the whole shopping experience and leads to higher conversion rates. Product classification and shelf monitoring are two examples of the kinds of jobs that may be automated with the use of image recognition technology for merchants.

Analytics Predictive of Trends in the Market

For the purpose of identifying new trends and consumer preferences, artificial intelligence and machine learning algorithms scan social media, customer reviews, and other sources of unstructured data. This knowledge may be used by retailers in order to forecast customer demand and adjust their product offers appropriately.

The Identification and Prevention of Fraud

Transaction data is analyzed by machine learning algorithms in order to identify fraudulent behaviors such as identity theft and payment counterfeiting. Retailers have the ability to secure their customers' sensitive information and minimize financial losses by recognizing suspicious trends in real time.

The production area

Automation, predictive maintenance, and quality control are achieved in industrial processes via the use of AI and ML technology. The purpose of these technologies is to optimize production schedules, eliminate downtime, and maintain product quality by analyzing sensor data, production records, and the operation of equipment. The use of artificial intelligence and machine learning in the production sector of industries is not only a trend; rather, it is a must for maintaining competitiveness and efficiency in the contemporary market. These technological advancements provide a broad variety of advantages, including the enhancement of efficiency and quality, as well as the improvement of safety and sustainability. AI and ML will continue to develop, which will result in an increase in their involvement in production, which will in turn drive additional breakthroughs and innovation across a variety of sectors.

Modes of transportation

The technology behind driverless vehicles relies heavily on artificial intelligence and machine learning. In order to navigate and make judgments in real time, self-driving vehicles employ sophisticated algorithms to evaluate input from sensors, cameras, and global positioning systems (GPS). These technologies improve safety by lowering the likelihood of errors caused by humans, optimizing routes, and enhancing the flow of traffic. In the transportation industry, the demand for artificial intelligence and machine learning is driven by the pursuit of improved user experience, safety, and efficiency. From driverless cars and predictive maintenance to route optimization and tailored services, these technologies are bringing about a transformation in every facet of the sector. In the future, artificial intelligence and machine learning will have a greater influence on transportation, which will result in transportation systems that are more intelligent, safer, and more efficient.

Energy

It is via the optimization of energy production, distribution, and consumption that AI and ML are bringing about a transformation in the energy industry. The purpose of these technologies is to improve dependability and save costs by analyzing sensor data from power grids, optimizing renewable energy sources, and predicting equipment breakdowns. Improvements in efficiency, dependability, and sustainability are being driven by artificial intelligence and machine learning, which are becoming important in the energy business. These technologies are causing a transformation in the manner in which energy is generated, delivered, and consumed. These technologies include predictive maintenance and smart grids, as well as the optimization of renewable energy and the reduction of emissions. As artificial intelligence and machine learning continue to advance, their influence on the energy industry will increase, which will result in an energy landscape that is more robust, efficient, and environmentally friendly.

Communication and Information Technology

It is possible to enhance the performance and dependability of a network by using AI and ML algorithms. It is possible for them to forecast and monitor network traffic, identify bottlenecks, and dynamically distribute resources in order to keep performance at its highest possible level. This results in improved user experiences and less downtime for the system. It is essential to improve cybersecurity to make use of AI and ML. By studying patterns and irregularities in network traffic, these technologies are able to identify and react to threats in real time. Machine learning models have the ability to recognize new forms of malware and phishing attempts, which enables them to provide proactive defensive mechanisms and reduce the chance of security breaches. It is the pursuit of increased efficiency, higher security, and improved user experiences that is driving the demand for artificial intelligence and machine learning in the communication and information technology industries. These technologies are causing a revolution in every facet of the business, from the optimization of networks and the protection of data to the provision of individualized services and the implementation of intelligent automation. The influence that AI and ML have on communication and information technology will continue to rise as they continue to develop, which will result in solutions that are more inventive, dependable, and user-friendly.

Agriculture

Through allowing precision farming, crop monitoring, and yield prediction, artificial intelligence and machine learning technologies are transforming the agricultural industry. Satellite imaging, meteorological data, and soil conditions are all analysed by these technologies in order to maximize the use of available resources, boost agricultural yields, and reduce the negative effect on the environment. Through the provision of data-driven insights into a variety of agricultural tasks, artificial intelligence and machine learning make precision farming possible. By evaluating data collected from sensors, drones, and satellites, these technologies provide assistance to farmers in making educated choices on planting, fertilizing, and harvesting their crops. This results in greater agricultural yields, less material waste, and optimal use of available resources. The desire to improve production, efficiency, and sustainability in agriculture is the driving force behind the use of artificial intelligence and machine learning. Precision farming, crop health monitoring, irrigation management, and supply chain optimization are just some of the many possible applications for these technologies, which provide a broad variety of advantages. They will have a greater influence on agriculture as artificial intelligence and machine learning continue to progress, which will result in agricultural techniques that are more inventive and sustainable, which will allow them to face the difficulties of feeding a rising global population.

Entertainment and the Media Field

When it comes to the media and entertainment sector, artificial intelligence and machine learning improve content development,

Applications of Artificial Intelligence and Machine Learning
audience engagement, and content suggestion. Through the
analysis of user preferences, viewing patterns, and interactions on
social media, these technologies are able to provide users with
tailored content and enhance their overall experiences.

Content Creation and Production

Artificial intelligence and machine learning are bringing about a
revolution in the production and development of content by
automating and improving a variety of processes:

Storytelling & Scriptwriting: Artificial intelligence systems have
the ability to produce narrative ideas, provide assistance in
scriptwriting, and even forecast how audiences would respond to
certain plotlines. For writers and producers, this makes it easier
to generate material that is captivating and engaging.

Video Editing: Tools that are driven by artificial intelligence
provide the ability to automate processes like as cutting,
transitions, and color correction, which helps save time and
improves the overall quality of the production.

VFX stands for visual effects, and machine learning algorithms
have the ability to make realistic VFX. This includes the creation
of virtual environments and the de-aging of performers. Because
of this, manufacturing time and expenses are reduced.

Individualization and Suggestions for Improvement

Personalization that is powered by artificial intelligence is
essential to improving the user experience in the entertainment
and media industries:

Content suggestions: Machine learning algorithms are used by streaming services such as Netflix and Spotify to monitor user behavior and preferences in order to provide tailored content suggestions of its users. The engagement and pleasure of users is increased as a result.

Adjustment of the Content Dynamically: Artificial intelligence has the ability to personalize material in real time depending on how users engage with it. A good example of something that keeps people interested is the usage of tailored news feeds and customized marketing messaging.

Conducting Audience Research and Targeting

It is essential for the media business to have a solid understanding of the tastes and habits of the audience:

The analysis of sentiment: The public's feelings on material, celebrities, or events may be analyzed by artificial intelligence via the use of social media and other internet platforms. Decisions about marketing and content development may be made more effectively with the aid of this information.

A Segmentation of the Audience: The use of machine learning algorithms enables the segmentation of audiences according to demographics, tastes, and behaviours, which in turn enables targeted marketing and providing tailored information.

As a result of the desire to improve efficiency, customization, and user experience, artificial intelligence and machine learning are

Applications of Artificial Intelligence and Machine Learning becoming more popular in the entertainment and media sectors. The development of content, the study of audiences, the moderation of material, and predictive analytics are just some of the many advantages that may be gained by using these technologies. In the future, artificial intelligence and machine learning will have a greater influence on the entertainment and media industries, which will result in audiences all over the globe having experiences that are more inventive, engaging, and individualized.

Instructional Methods

AI and ML are being used in the field of education for the purposes of individualized learning, adaptive assessments, and student support systems. Pupils' data, learning habits, and performance indicators are analyzed by these technologies, which allows for the customization of educational experiences, the identification of pupils who are at risk, and the provision of tailored interventions. Through the incorporation of Artificial Intelligence (AI) and Machine Learning (ML) into instructional techniques, education is undergoing a transformation that is characterized by the enhancement of teaching effectiveness, the personalization of learning experiences, and the improvement of administrative efficiency. The desire to improve customization, efficiency, and engagement in education is the driving force behind the implementation of artificial intelligence and machine learning in instructional approaches. Some of the many advantages that may be gained by using these technologies include individualized learning and intelligent tutoring, as well as automated grading and predictive analytics. The continued development of artificial intelligence and machine learning will have an increasing influence on the techniques of teaching, which will result in educational experiences that are more efficient, inclusive, and inventive for both students and teachers.

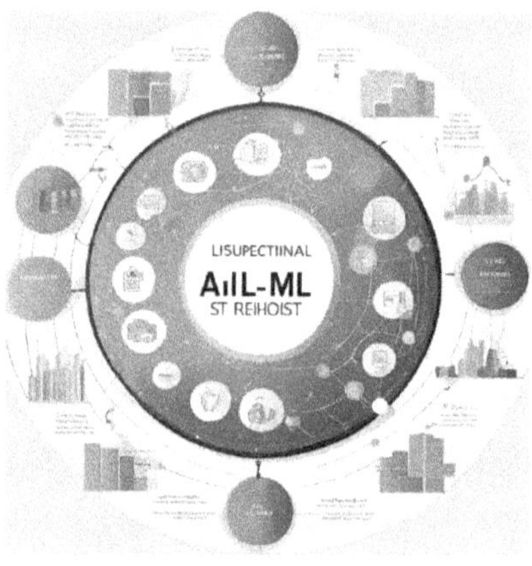

Figure. 1.8 Instructional Methods

1.3. Fundamental Concepts of AI

Artificial intellect (AI) is the area of computer science that seeks to develop computers that can carry out activities that normally require human intellect. Reasoning, learning, problem-solving, perception, language comprehension, and decision-making are some of these activities.

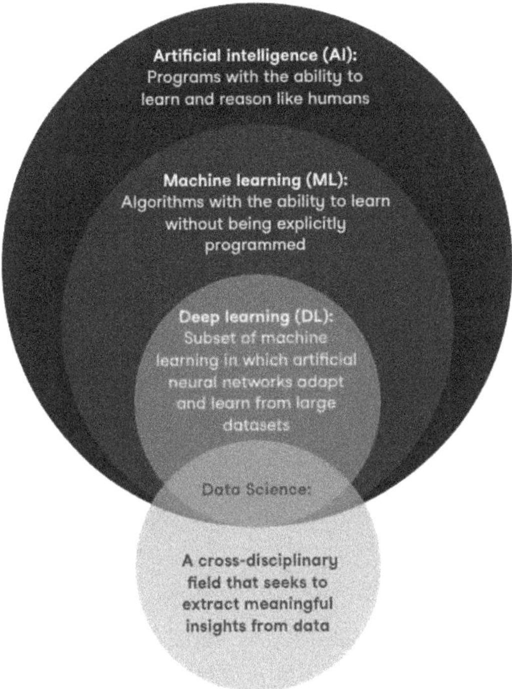

Figure. 1.9 Fundamental Concepts of AI

Types of AI

Narrow AI (Weak AI)

Weak AI, or narrow AI, describes artificial intelligence (AI) systems that are taught and intended to do a narrow range of tasks. These systems are limited in what they can do and can only function within the parameters that have been specified for them. In today's technological world, narrow AI, also known as weak AI, is essential since it provides specialized solutions that increase production and efficiency across a range of sectors. Although it is quite good at some jobs, its shortcomings show how difficult it is to develop AI systems that are more flexible and adaptable.

Leveraging the possibilities of Narrow AI efficiently and ethically requires an understanding of its limitations as well as its benefits.

Figure. 1.10 Narrow AI (Weak AI)

General AI (Strong AI)

General artificial intelligence (AI) is a form of artificial intelligence that can comprehend, absorb, and apply knowledge across a broad variety of tasks at a level equivalent to human intellect. It is sometimes referred to as Strong AI or Artificial General Intelligence (AGI). Whereas Narrow AI is tailored to certain activities, General AI seeks to do every intellectual job that a person is capable of. The goal of creating computers with human-like intelligence and adaptability is known as general artificial intelligence (AI). Although it has the potential to revolutionize many facets of society, putting it into practice will present substantial ethical, social, and technological obstacles. Comprehending the basic principles of artificial intelligence (AI)

Applications of Artificial Intelligence and Machine Learning aids in acknowledging its intricacy and the significant influence it may have on the trajectory of technology and human existence in the future.

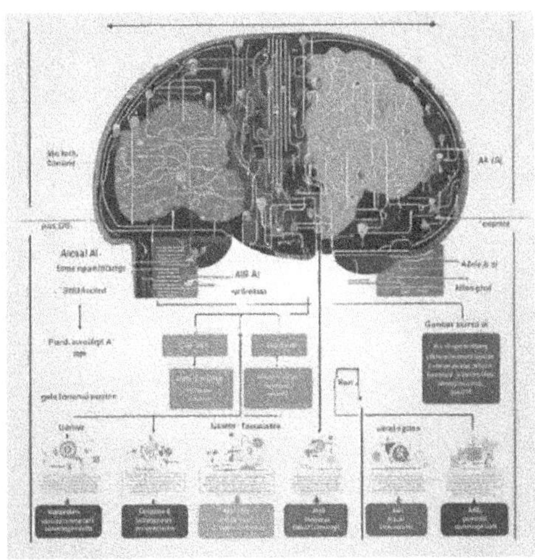

Figure. 1.11 Narrow AI (Weak AI) and General AI (Strong AI)

Super intelligent AI

A hypothetical artificial intelligence system known as "super intelligent AI" is said to be more intelligent than humans in all areas, including creativity, problem-solving, emotional intelligence, and social abilities. Super intelligent AI would be much more advanced than Narrow AI, which is made for specialized tasks, and General AI, which seeks to emulate human-level intellect in a variety of disciplines. With powers well beyond those of humans, super intelligent AI is the potential peak of artificial intelligence. Although it has enormous promise to improve human welfare, science, and technology, it also presents serious hazards and obstacles that need to be properly controlled. Navigating the intricate and quickly changing field of AI research and development requires an understanding of the principles and applications of super intelligent AI.

Figure. 1.12 Super intelligent AI

Key Components of AI

- Machine Learning (ML): This branch of AI deals with teaching algorithms to learn from and forecast data.

- Natural Language Processing (NLP): The capacity of artificial intelligence to comprehend, translate, and produce human language.

- Computer Vision: This enables AI to analyze and comprehend visual data from the outside world, including pictures and movies.

Applications of Artificial Intelligence and Machine Learning

- Robotics: combining artificial intelligence with real robots to carry out tasks on their own.

AI Techniques

- Rule-Based Systems: AI programs that carry out activities based on pre-established rules and logic.

- Heuristic Search: AI methods that investigate potential solutions in order to identify the optimal one; often used to optimization issues and game play.

- Expert Systems: AI programs that use a knowledge base and inference rules to simulate a human expert's decision-making process.

1.4. Fundamental Concepts of ML

A branch of artificial intelligence called machine learning (ML) focuses on creating algorithms that let computers learn from data and make judgments or predictions without explicit programming.

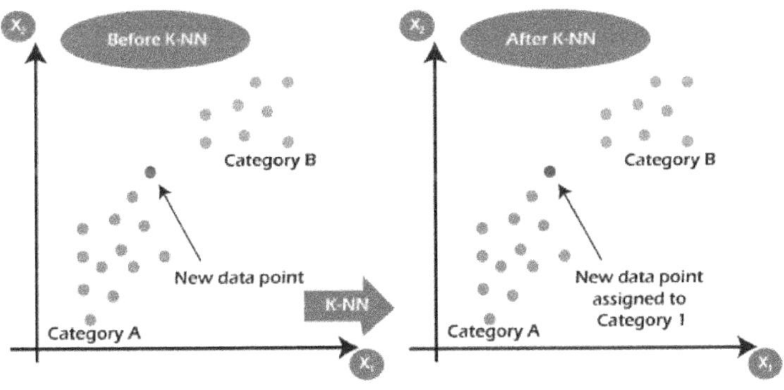

Figure. 1.13 Fundamental Concepts of ML

Types of ML

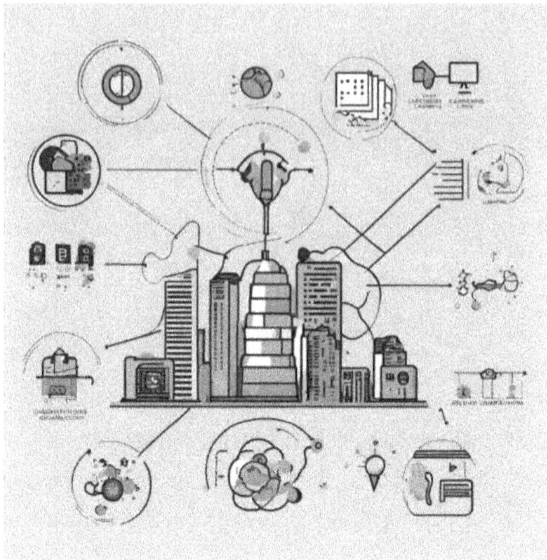

Figure. 1.14 Types of ML

Supervised Learning

Every training sample in the labeled dataset that the algorithm is trained on has an output label associated with it. Finding a mapping from inputs to outputs is the aim.

Unsupervised Learning

The algorithm must identify patterns or structure in the incoming data because it was trained on an unlabeled dataset.

Semi-Supervised Learning

Uses a huge quantity of unlabeled data combined with a limited amount of labeled data for training. When classifying data requires a lot of money or effort, this is helpful.

Reinforcement Learning

Applications of Artificial Intelligence and Machine Learning Through interaction with its surroundings and feedback in the form of incentives or punishments, the algorithm gains knowledge. Finding a policy that optimizes cumulative rewards is the aim.

Key Components of ML

- Databases: A grouping of data used to test and train machine learning models. Data quantity and quality are essential to the functioning of the model.

- Features: The distinct, quantifiable qualities or traits of the data that the algorithm uses to learn.

- Models: The learning process represented mathematically. After being educated on data, models are used to forecast or make choices.

- Algorithms: The processes or equations the model employs to draw conclusions from data and provide forecasts. Neural networks, decision trees, and support vector machines are a few examples.

ML Techniques

- Regression: Using input feature information to predict a continuous output variable.

- Classification: Putting incoming data into one of several established groups.

- Clustering: Assembling comparable data points without assigned labels.

- Dimensionality reduction: lowering the total number of input variables while maintaining the necessary level of detail in the model.

- Neural Networks: Computer systems that are modeled after the neural networks found in the human brain; especially useful for intricate pattern recognition applications.

- Deep Learning: A branch of machine learning that uses multi-layered neural networks (deep neural networks) and is especially useful for voice and picture recognition.

Though their principles are different, AI and ML are linked sciences. While machine learning (ML) focuses on constructing algorithms that let systems learn from data, artificial intelligence (AI) focuses on building systems that behave intelligently. Gaining an understanding of these core ideas paves the way for investigating and using AI and ML technologies in a variety of sectors.

1.5. Concept of Deep Learning in AI and ML

Multi-layered neural networks are used in deep learning, a kind of machine learning, to model and comprehend intricate patterns seen in huge datasets. By simulating how the human brain processes information, these neural networks enable robots to recognize patterns, reach choices, and gain experience.

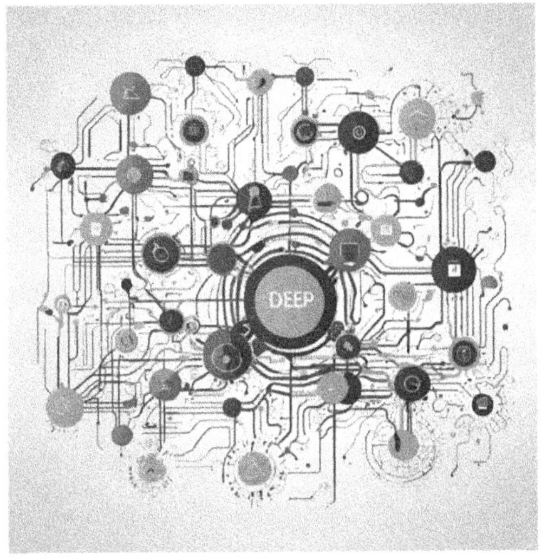

Figure. 1.15 Concept of Deep Learning in AI and ML

Essential Elements of Deep Learning

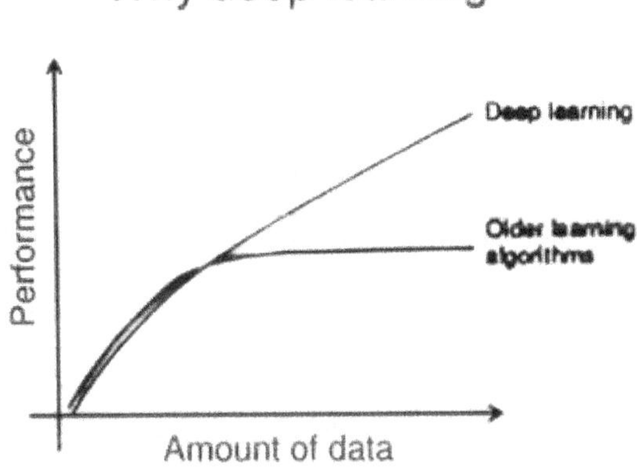

Figure. 1.16 Concept of Deep Learning

Neural Networks

Neural nets are the core of deep learning. These are made up of layers upon layers of nodes, or neurons, interconnected with one another. While convolutional neural networks (CNNs) are used for image processing and recurrent neural networks (RNNs) are used for sequential data, feedforward neural networks are the most fundamental form.

Layers

- Input Layer: The first layer, via which data is added to the network.
- Hidden Layers: intermediate layers that extract characteristics and patterns from the raw data as they analyze it. Several hidden layers are usually involved in deep learning, thus the name "deep."
- Output Layer: The final layer, which generates output for the network.

Activation Functions

Functions that are added to a neuron's input to provide non-linearity to the model and help the network recognize intricate patterns. Tanh, sigmoid, and ReLU (Rectified Linear Unit) are examples of common activation functions.

Training

The process of changing the network's weights in order to reduce prediction error. Usually, an optimization approach like gradient descent is used in conjunction with a backpropagation technique.

Loss Function

Applications of Artificial Intelligence and Machine Learning
The process of changing the network's weights in order to reduce prediction error. Usually, an optimization approach like gradient descent is used in conjunction with a backpropagation technique.

Applications of Deep Learning

- Image and Video Recognition: For applications including object identification, face recognition, and picture categorization, CNNs are often used.
- Natural Language Processing (NLP): Text creation, sentiment analysis, and language translation are applications for models such as RNNs and transformers.
- Speech Recognition: Deep learning models are employed in transcription services and virtual assistants because they can comprehend and transcribe human speech.
- Autonomous Vehicles: For tasks like object identification, route planning, and decision making in autonomous vehicles, deep learning is essential.
- Healthcare: Used for illness outbreak prediction, medicine development, and medical image analysis.
- Advantages of Deep Learning
- High Accuracy: Particularly when working with big datasets, deep learning models often outperform conventional machine learning models in terms of accuracy.
- Automatic Feature Extraction: Deep learning algorithms automatically extract useful features from

raw data, in contrast to standard models that need human feature extraction.

- Scalability: The performance of deep learning models may be enhanced by scaling them with additional data and processing capacity.

Challenges of Deep Learning

- Data Requirements: To function successfully, deep learning models usually need a lot of labeled data.

- Computational Resources: Deep learning model training requires a lot of resources; strong GPUs and a lot of processing time are often needed.

- Interpretability: Deep learning models are notoriously difficult to comprehend, frequently being seen as "black boxes" because of their intricacy.

In artificial intelligence and machine learning, deep learning is a potent and quickly developing discipline. It is appropriate for a variety of applications because to its capacity to manage enormous volumes of data and identify complex patterns. Deep learning continues to attract a lot of attention and investment despite its difficulties because of its potential advantages.

2. Generation of AI /ML for Application

The "generation of AI/ML for application" refers to the process of developing, implementing, and utilizing machine learning (ML) and artificial intelligence (AI) models to address real-world issues in specific applications. This entails a number of methodical procedures to convert unprocessed data into instruments for automated decision-making and actionable insights.

The process of developing and using machine learning and artificial intelligence models to tackle certain challenges or activities within a given field is known as "generation of AI/ML for application." This involves formulating issues, processing data, building models, assessing them, and deploying them seamlessly into new or existing applications to enhance functionality, efficiency, and decision-making skills.

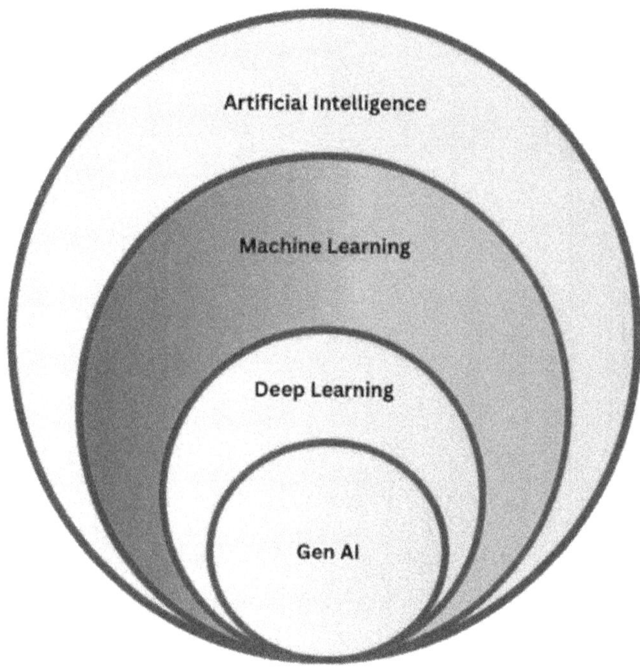

Figure.2.1 Generation of AI /ML for application

2.1 Problem Definition in the Generation of AI/ML for Applications

The first and most important stage in creating AI/ML for applications is the issue description phase. It entails defining precisely the issue that has to be solved and laying out the framework for the whole AI/ML development process. This stage guarantees that the work is in line with the goals of the company or the research and that the AI/ML model will provide useful and actionable results.

Figure.2.2 Problem Definition in the Generation of AI/ML for Applications

Objective Identification

- Company Objective: Specify the main aim of the study or company. For instance, boosting client retention rates, anticipating equipment malfunctions, or streamlining customer service.

- AI/ML Task: Indicate the kind of job, e.g., recommendation, grouping, regression, classification, etc.

Scope and Constraints

- Scope: Define the parameters of the issue. What will the project contain and what won't?

- Limitations: Determine any restrictions, including those related to data accessibility, computing capacity, time restraints, legal mandates, or financial resources.

Stakeholders

- Participation: List every stakeholder that the AI/ML application will affect. End users, corporate executives, data scientists, and IT staff are all included in this.

- Requirements: Collect requirements from relevant parties to make sure the solution satisfies their expectations.

Success Metrics

- Establish the measurements that will be used to evaluate the effectiveness of the AI/ML solution by defining the key performance indicators (KPIs). Accuracy, precision, recall, F1 score, RMSE, and business-specific KPIs like more revenue or lower expenses are a few examples of these.

- Baseline Performance: To comprehend the existing situation and establish goals for improvement, establish baseline performance levels.

Data Requirements

- Data Sources: List and explain the sources of the information that will be consulted. Databases, APIs, logs, and external datasets may be examples of this.

- Features of the Data: Recognize the characteristics of the data, such as its volume, diversity, velocity, and accuracy.

Applications of Artificial Intelligence and Machine Learning
Sort the data according to its structure: structured, semi-structured, or unstructured.

- Evaluate the data's quality, taking into account its correctness, completeness, and any biases.

Example of Problem Definition

Example: Predicting Customer Churn in a Subscription Service

Objective Identification

- Business Objective: Lower customer attrition by identifying those who are most likely to discontinue their membership.
- Task using AI and machine learning: classifying data to forecast churn (binary classification: churn or no churn).

Scope and Constraints

- Scope: Pay attention to those who are currently using the service; those who have previously canceled are not included.
- Limitations: Limited access to previous data; adherence to data privacy laws (e.g., GDPR).

Stakeholders

- Marketing group, customer service, data scientists, and IT division are all involved.
- Requirements: The model must provide useful insights, such risky client categories and churn-causing variables.

Success Metrics

- Key Performance Indicators: F1 score, recall, accuracy, precision, and decrease in churn rate after the use of focused interventions.
- Baseline: There is a 15% turnover rate at the moment.

Data Requirements

- Data sources include use statistics, survey results, customer interaction logs, and CRM databases.
- Features of the Data: Customer demographics, subscription information, use trends, and customer service exchanges are all included in the data.
- Data quality: Make sure the information is correct, current, and devoid of major biases.
- A clear path for the AI/ML project is established by a well-defined issue description, which also ensures alignment with corporate objectives, comprehends stakeholder demands, and establishes success criteria. This fundamental stage assists in generating a targeted and efficient AI/ML solution that handles the particular challenge successfully.

2.2. Data Collection and Preparation in the Generation of AI/ML for Applications

An essential first step in creating AI/ML models is gathering and preparing data. The performance and dependability of the AI/ML systems are directly impacted by these procedures, which guarantee that the data used to train and assess the models is accurate, relevant, and presented appropriately.

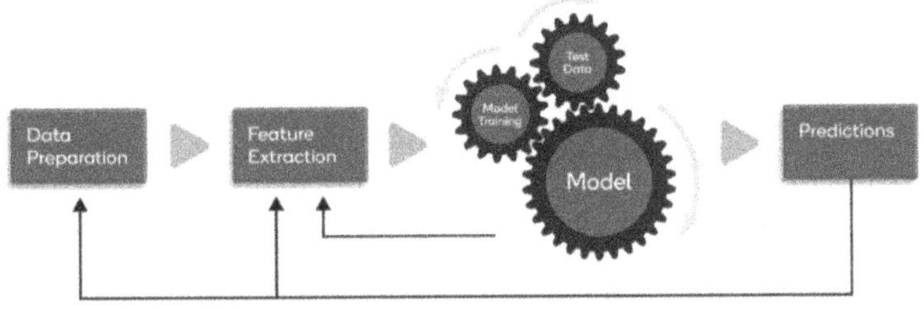

Figure.2.3 Data Collection and Preparation in the Generation of AI/ML for Applications

Data Collection

Identify Data Sources

- Internal Data: User-generated content, transaction records, CRM systems, databases, and logs.
- External Data: online scraping, public datasets, APIs, and third-party data sources.
- Data Types
- Tabular data in databases or spreadsheets (sales records, sensor data, etc.) is referred to as structured data.
- Unstructured data includes text, photos, audio, and video (such as emails and postings on social media).
- Semi-structured Data: HTML, XML, JSON (such as metadata and web APIs).

Data Collection Methods

- Using web scraping tools, APIs, sensors, scripts, or other automated data collection methods.
- Human data entry, often performed when automated data collecting is not practical.

- Crowdsourcing: Gathering information from a large number of individuals, usually via websites such as Amazon Mechanical Turk.
- Data Collection Considerations
- Volume: The necessary amount of data.
- Velocity: The velocity at which information is created and gathered.
- Variety: Various data kinds and sources.
- Veracity: Data dependability and accuracy.

Data Preparation

Data Cleaning

- Removing missing data, imputing missing values using the mean, median, and mode, or using algorithms designed to handle missing values are some methods for handling missing values.
- Eliminating Duplicates: Locating and eliminating redundant entries.
- Error correction: repairing erroneous data entry (such as typos and mislabeled information).

Data Transformation

- Scaling numerical data to a conventional range, such as 0-1, is known as normalization.
- Data are adjusted to have a mean of 0 and a standard deviation of 1. This is known as standardization.

Applications of Artificial Intelligence and Machine Learning

- Encoding Categorical Data: Using methods like one-hot encoding or label encoding, categorical variables are transformed into numerical values.

- Feature engineering is the process of generating new features (such as interaction terms and date components) from already-existing data in order to enhance model performance.

Data Splitting

- Training Set: Usually consists of 70–80% of the data and is used to train the model.

- Validation Set: Usually 10-15% of the data, used to validate the model and adjust hyper parameters during training.

- Test Set: Usually 10-15% of the total data, used to assess the performance of the final model.

- Data Augmentation (for image, audio, text)

- Image augmentation methods include color correction, scaling, rotation, and flipping.

- Pitch-shifting, time-shifting, and adding noise are among methods used in audio augmentation.

- Techniques for text augmentation include back translation, random insertion, and synonym substitution.

- Example Workflow: Predicting Customer Churn in a Subscription Service

- Data Collection

- Determine Data Sources: Internal CRM system for use statistics, survey answers, customer information, and interaction logs.

- Two types of data exist: unstructured data (emails from customer support) and structured data (membership information).

Data Preparation

Data Cleaning:

- For numerical characteristics, the median value should be used for imputing, and for categorical features, the most common value should be used.
- Eliminate redundant customer interaction records.
- Fix data entry mistakes such dates that are off or categories that aren't labeled correctly.

Data Transformation:

- Normalize numerical attributes such as frequency of use, age, and wealth.
- Categorical variables, such customer segment and subscription type, may be encoded once.
- Incorporate fresh elements such as tenure, which measures the gap between the start and end dates of a subscription.

Data Splitting:

To achieve robust model assessment, divide data into three categories: seventy percent training, fifteen percent validation, and fifteen percent test sets.

Tools and Libraries

Applications of Artificial Intelligence and Machine Learning

- Gathering data: SQL, REST, Graph APIs, and site scraping programs (Scrapy, BeautifulSoup).

- NumPy, Open Refine, Pandas are tools for cleaning and transforming data.

- Tensor Flow, Keras, Augmentations for photos; Audiomentations for audio; NLPaug for text are examples of data augmentation tools.

2.3. Model Selection and Development in the Generation of AI/ML for Applications

When developing AI/ML applications, model selection and development are crucial stages when the right algorithms are selected, models are constructed, and performance is maximized to solve the specified challenge. In order to make that the chosen model meets the intended performance criteria and solves the issue successfully, this phase entails a number of crucial activities.

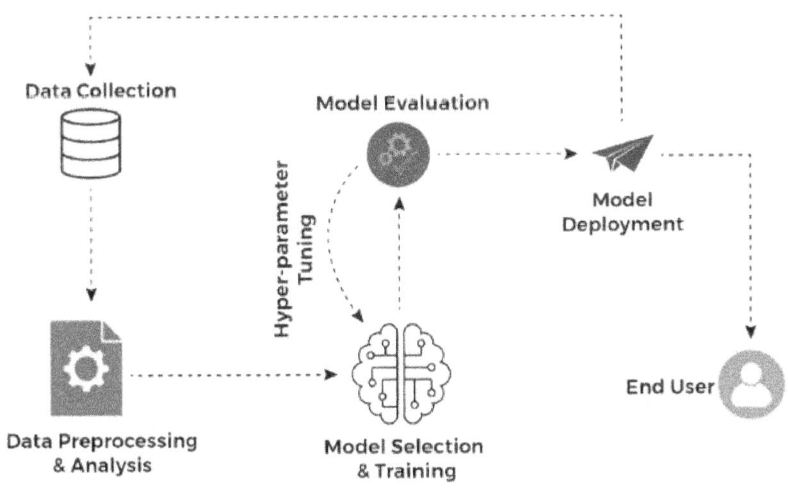

Figure.2.4 Data Collection and Preparation in the Generation of AI/ML for Applications

Model Selection

Understand the Problem Type

- Classification: Assist with picture identification and spam detection by forecasting category labels.
- Predict continuous values using regression (e.g., property prices, stock prices).
- Sort data points into clusters using the clustering technique (e.g., customer segmentation).
- Make recommendations for goods or courses of action (e.g., content suggestions, product recommendations).
- Time series forecasting (e.g., sales forecasting): anticipate future values based on historical data.
- Consider Algorithm Characteristics
- Complexity vs. Simplicity: Simple models (like decision trees and linear regression) against complicated models (like neural networks and ensemble techniques).
- Interpretability: Black-box models (like deep learning) vs models that provide light on the significance of features (like logistic regression and decision trees).
- Scalability: Models (e.g., distributed deep learning frameworks, gradient boosting machines) with the capacity to handle big datasets effectively.
- Training Time: Take into account how long it will take to train the model, particularly for big datasets.

Common Algorithms

Applications of Artificial Intelligence and Machine Learning

- Classification techniques include Support Vector Machines, Neural Networks (CNNs, RNNs), Gradient Boosting (Boost, LightGBM), Decision Trees, Random Forests, and Logistic Regression.

- Regression: Neural networks, decision trees, random forests, gradient boosting, linear regression, and ridge/lasso regression.

- Clustering techniques include Gaussian mixture models, DBSCAN, K-means, and hierarchical clustering.

- Neural collaborative filtering, content-based filtering, matrix factorization, collaborative filtering, and content-based filtering are recommended.

- Forecasting time series using ARIMA, Prophet, LSTM, and GRU.

- Pre-trained Models and Transfer Learning

- Pre-trained models (e.g., ResNet, BERT, and GPT) and transfer learning may dramatically shorten training times and boost performance for applications including image recognition, natural language processing, and voice recognition.

Model Development

Data Preprocessing

- Make that the data is standardized and in the right format, as needed by the chosen method.

- To generate new, relevant features and enhance model performance, use feature engineering.

Model Training

- Training: Fit the model using the training dataset.
- Hyperparameter tuning: Apply methods such as grid search, random search, or Bayesian optimization to optimize hyperparameters.
- Cross-validation: To make sure the model adapts effectively to new data, use k-fold cross-validation.

Model Evaluation

- Validation Set: Use the validation set to test the model in order to adjust hyperparameters and avoid overfitting.
- Metrics: Utilize the proper assessment metrics according to the nature of the issue (e.g., RMSE, MAE for regression; accuracy, precision, recall, F1 score for classification).
- Confusion Matrix: Examine the confusion matrix to determine the kinds of mistakes the model is producing in classification issues (e.g., false positives, false negatives).

Model Improvement

- Feature engineering: To improve model performance, iteratively tweak features.
- Algorithm tuning involves experimenting with various algorithms or ensemble approaches (combinations of algorithms).
- Regularization: To avoid overfitting, use strategies like dropout and L1, L2 regularization for neural networks.

Model Validation

- Cross-Validation: To evaluate the model's performance more thoroughly, use methods like k-fold cross-validation.

Applications of Artificial Intelligence and Machine Learning

- Bootstrapping: Resample data using a replacement in order to gauge the model's precision and unpredictability.

- Model Deployment

- Exporting the Model: Save the learned model in a deployment-ready format (such as PMML, ONNX, or Tensor Flow Saved Model).

- Making APIs Create APIs to make the model available by using frameworks such as Flask and Fast API.

- Integration: Incorporate the model into the program, making sure it works well with current systems.

- Scalability: Use cloud services (such as AWS Sage Maker and Google AI Platform) to make sure the model can manage the anticipated demand.

- Example Workflow: Predicting Customer Churn in a Subscription Service

Model Selection

- Recognize the Type of Issue: This is an issue with categorization (churn or no churn).

- Think about algorithms. Features: Pick algorithms that strike a balance between performance and interpretability. For interpretability, start with logistic regression; for better performance, take into account more sophisticated models like random forests, gradient boosting, or neural networks.

Model Development

Data Preprocessing:

- Normalize numerical attributes such as tenure and use frequency.
- Categorical characteristics like client segment and subscription type may be encoded once.

Model Training:

- Build a baseline model for logistic regression training.
- Learn more sophisticated models, such as gradient boosting and random forests.
- Adjust the hyperparameters by using random or grid search.
- Model Evaluation:
- Model evaluation metrics include accuracy, precision, recall, and F1 score.
- Confusion matrix analysis may be used to find frequent misclassifications.

Model Improvement:

- Add polynomial and interaction terms to features to refine them.
- Try out group techniques such as blending or stacking.
- Model Validation:
- Verify the model's good generalization by using k-fold cross-validation.
- To measure the accuracy and variability of a model, use bootstrapping.

Model Deployment

- Exporting the Model: Save the model with the best performance in a format that works for it (job lib for scikit-learn models, for example).

- Building APIs: Use Flask to create RESTful APIs that provide the model predictions.

- Integration: To deliver churn forecasts in real time, integrate the model with the CRM system.

- Scalability: Use a scalable cloud platform, such as AWS Sage Maker, to deploy the model.

Tools and Libraries

- The following models were chosen and developed: TensorFlow, Py Torch, XG Boost, Light GBM, and Scikit-learn.

- Preprocessing data using Pandas and NumPy.

- Hyperopt, Scikit-learn, and Optuna for hyperparameter tuning.

- Model evaluation using MLflow and Scikit-learn.

- Flask, Fast API, Docker, Kubernetes, AWS Sage Maker, and Google AI Platform are some of the models that are deployed.

- Iterative and dynamic processes, model selection and development need a thorough comprehension of the issue, data, and available techniques. You may develop reliable AI/ML systems that successfully address real-world issues by methodically choosing, training, and assessing models, and then deploying them in a scalable and maintainable way.

2.4. Model Evaluation and Tuning in the Generation of AI/ML for Applications

Model assessment and tuning are critical phases in the creation and use of machine learning (ML) and artificial intelligence (AI) models. These procedures guarantee that models operate at peak efficiency and satisfy the particular needs of their intended uses. Below, we provide an outline of these ideas, methods, and recommendations.

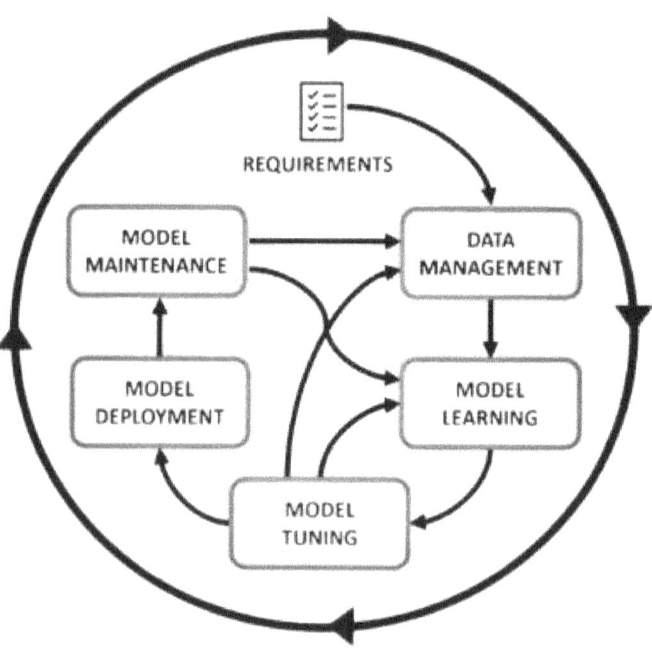

Figure. 2.5 Model Evaluation and Tuning in the Generation of AI/ML for Applications

Model Evaluation

Applications of Artificial Intelligence and Machine Learning

In order to make sure a machine learning model satisfies the required levels of accuracy, dependability, and generalizability, it must be evaluated. Important measures and procedures for evaluating a model include:

Train-Test Split:

- Training Set: The model is trained using this set.
- Testing Set: Used to assess how well the model performs with untested data.

Cross-Validation:

- K-Fold Cross-Validation: The dataset is split up into K subsets. The model is trained and verified K times, using the remaining subsets as the training set and a different subset as the validation set each time.
- Stratified cross-validation: This technique, which is particularly helpful for unbalanced datasets, makes sure that each fold has a comparable class distribution.

Evaluation Metrics:

- The proportion of accurately anticipated cases to all occurrences is known as accuracy.
- F1-score, recall, and precision: The precision measures the proportion of accurate positive predictions to all positive predictions. The ratio of all real positives to all genuine positive forecasts is known as recall. The harmonic mean of recall and accuracy is known as the F1-Score.
- A table that contrasts real and anticipated data to show how well a categorization model performs.

- The receiver operating characteristic-area under the curve, or ROC-AUC, assesses how well the model can differentiate between classes.
- Common metrics for regression models include Mean Absolute Error (MAE), Mean Squared Error (MSE), and Root Mean Squared Error (RMSE).

Overfitting and under fitting:

- When a model does well on training data but badly on testing data, it is said to be overfitting. It shows that the training data included noise and information that the model did not adequately generalize.
- When a model behaves badly on both training and testing data, it is said to be under fitting. It suggests that the model is not sophisticated enough to fully represent the underlying patterns in the data.

Model Tuning

Model tuning is the process of fine-tuning a model's hyper parameters to increase performance. Important methods consist of:

Grid Search:

- A thorough search across a given parameter grid is defined.
- The process involves evaluating every conceivable combination of hyper parameters and choosing the combination that performs the best.

Random Search:

- Definition: A search over arbitrary hyper parameter combinations.
- Procedure: Random sampling of hyper parameters is typically more efficient than grid search, particularly in cases when the hyper parameter space is huge.

Bayesian Optimization:

- Definition: An optimization method that selects the most promising hyper parameters to assess by creating a probabilistic model of the objective function.
- Benefit: more effective than random search and grid because it concentrates on regions of the hyper parameter space that should produce better results.

Gradient-Based Optimization:

Definition: Optimizes hyper parameters using gradients. Frequently employed in neural network training (e.g., momentum, learning rate).

Early Stopping:

Definition: It ends training when it notices a decline in the model's performance on a validation set, a sign that more training will cause overfitting.

Practical Considerations

Data Quality:

Make sure the training and assessment data is clear, well-prepared, and reflective of the actual environment in which the model will be applied.

Feature Engineering:

The procedure for adding new features or changing current ones in order to enhance model performance. The model's efficacy may be considerably impacted by this.

Model Interpretability:

Understanding and interpreting the model's predictions is essential in many applications. Complex models can be interpreted using methods such as SHAP (Shapley Additive explanations) and LIME (Local Interpretable Model-agnostic Explanations).

Computational Resources:

- Model assessment and hyper parameter adjustment might be computationally costly. Achieving a balance between the amount of computing resources available and the depth of tuning is crucial.
- Developing strong AI/ML applications requires careful consideration of both model evaluation and adjustment. Developers may construct models that fit unique demands of their applications, are generalizable, and perform effectively on real-world data by carefully evaluating model performance using relevant metrics and tuning hyper parameters.

2.5. Model Deployment in the Generation of AI/ML for Applications

The process of incorporating a machine learning (ML) model that has been trained into a production environment so that it may be utilized to forecast fresh data is known as model deployment. This phase is crucial because it moves the model from a research and development stage to practical applications. The following are the main ideas and recommended procedures for model deployment:

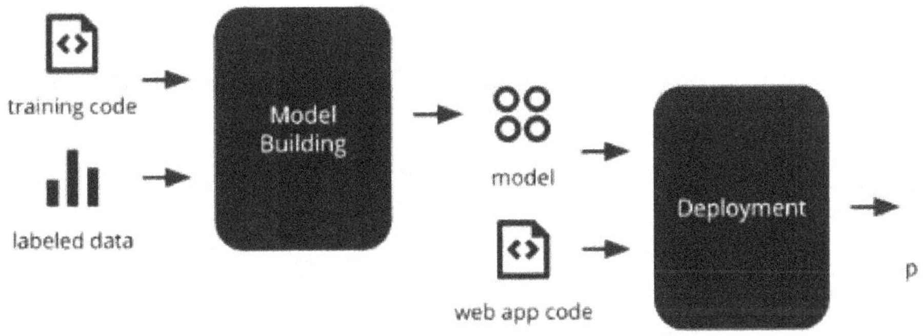

Figure. 2.6 Model Deployment in the Generation of AI/ML for Applications

Steps in Model Deployment

Model Packaging:

- The process of serialization involves transforming a model into a format that is simple to load and store. Pickle (Python), ONNX (Open Neural Network Exchange), and job lib are examples of common formats.

- Versioning is the process of managing changes and rolling back models by keeping track of their many iterations. Sustaining traceability and consistency requires this.

Infrastructure Setup:

- Deployment Environment: Depending on where the model will be deployed, this involves setting up the required infrastructure, such as edge devices, on-premises servers, or cloud services (AWS, Google Cloud, and Azure).
- Containerization: Creating a consistent runtime environment for the model with technologies like Docker to make sure it operates the same way in development, testing, and production.

Model Serving:

- Batch processing is appropriate in situations when real-time prediction is not required. Large amounts of data are processed by models at predetermined periods.
- Real-Time Serving: For applications like fraud detection or recommendation systems that need to make predictions right away. To service the model, RPC or REST APIs can be utilized.

Integration with Applications:

- APIs: By making the model available as an API, other apps may communicate with it. These APIs may be made using frameworks like Flask, Fast API, or Tensor Flow Serving.

- Database Integration: In order to get input data or store predictions, models may need to communicate with databases. It is essential to provide effective database access and data management.

Monitoring and Logging:

- Monitoring the model's performance in use to make sure it satisfies the necessary requirements is known as performance monitoring. It is important to keep an eye on metrics like error rates, throughput, and latency.

- Model Drift Detection: Constantly keeping an eye on the model's predictions to spot variations in the data distribution that can point to a declining level of model performance.

- Logging: To make debugging and performance analysis easier, logs for each prediction should be captured. This covers the input data, the forecasts, and any mistakes that were made.

Scaling:

Increasing the number of model instances to manage a growing demand is known as horizontal scaling. Several instances can receive requests from load balancers.

Vertical scaling is the process of giving the current infrastructure extra capacity by increasing its CPU and RAM.

Auto-scaling: Ensuring effective resource use by dynamically modifying the number of instances in accordance with the current demand.

Security:

Authentication and Authorization: Guaranteeing that the model can only be accessed by authorized users and apps.

Data encryption: preserving confidentiality and integrity by safeguarding data while it's in use and while it's at rest.

Compliance: Following applicable laws and guidelines, including the GDPR on data protection.

Best Practices

Continuous Integration and Continuous Deployment (CI/CD):

Automate the model-building, testing, and deployment processes. Pipelines for continuous integration and deployment may be set up using tools such as Circle CI, Git Lab CI/CD, and Jenkins.

A/B Testing:

Distributing many concurrent copies of the model to various user groups in order to assess performance and identify the optimal version.

Canary Deployment:

Before a large-scale implementation, the model should be gradually made available to a select group of consumers. This makes it easier to identify problems early on without harming all users.

Rollback Strategy:

Applications of Artificial Intelligence and Machine Learning

Preparing a fall back to the model's prior stable iteration in the event that the new deployment causes problems.

Documentation:

Keeping thorough records of the infrastructure configuration, model API, deployment procedure, and any dependencies. In the future, this will help in updating and maintaining the model.

Tools and Frameworks

ML flow:

An open-source framework for controlling the experimentation, repeatability, and deployment phases of machine learning.

Kube flow:

A production-ready infrastructure for ML model deployment, scaling, and management that runs on Kubernetes.

Tensor Flow Serving:

A flexible, high-performance serving system for deploying machine learning models, suited for production contexts.

Amazon Sage Maker:

A completely managed solution that makes it possible for any developer or data scientist to swiftly create, train, and implement machine learning models.

Google AI Platform:

A whole range of services for creating, implementing, and overseeing machine learning models.

2.6. Tools and Technologies in the Generation of AI/ML for Applications

A range of tools and technologies are used in the creation of AI/ML applications to support the many phases of the machine learning lifecycle, from model building and data preparation to deployment and monitoring. An overview of some of the most well-known instruments and technologies in the AI/ML space is provided below:

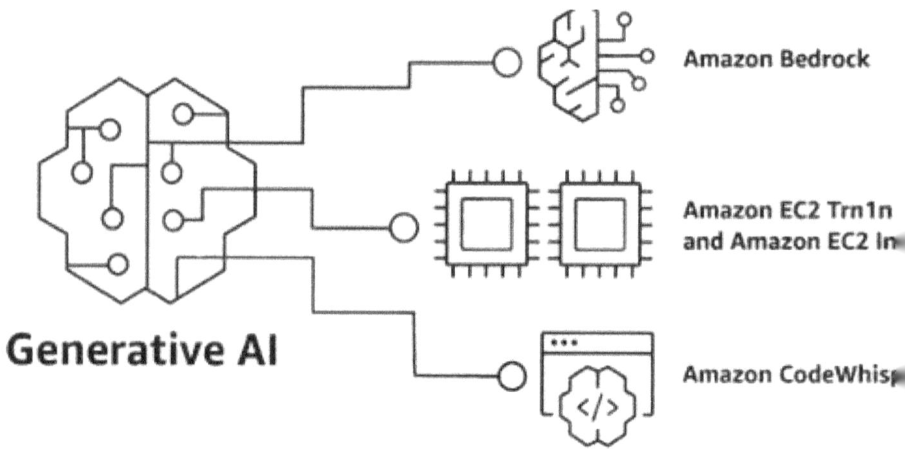

Figure. 2.7 Tools and Technologies in the Generation of AI/ML for Applications

Data Collection and Preparation

Pandas:

•	A Python data analysis and manipulation module. It offers the operations and data structures required to easily handle structured data.

NumPy:

•	A core Python module for scientific computing. Large, multidimensional arrays and matrices are supported, as well as a number of mathematical operations that may be performed on the arrays.

Apache Spark:

•	A fault-tolerant, implicitly data-parallel programming interface for whole clusters offered by an open-source distributed computing system.

Hadoop:

•	An open-source software framework that uses the MapReduce programming paradigm to handle and store massive amounts of data in a distributed manner.

Data Cleaning Libraries:

•	Open Refine: An effective tool for handling untidy data, allowing for format conversion and cleaning.

•	High hopes: a tool to verify, record, and profile data to make sure it's accurate.

Data Visualization

Matplotlib:

•	A complete Python visualization toolkit for static, animated, and interactive graphics creation.

Seaborn:

•	A Matplotlib-based Python visualization package that offers a high-level drawing interface for eye-catching statistical images.

Tableau:

•	An effective tool for data visualization that transforms unprocessed data into a comprehensible format.

Power BI:

•	A business analytics tool by Microsoft that provides interactive visualizations and business intelligence capabilities with an interface simple enough for end users to create their own reports and dashboards.

Model Development

Scikit-learn:

•	A machine learning library for Python that offers effective and user-friendly tools for data mining and analysis.

Tensor Flow:

•	A full-featured open-source machine learning platform created by Google that is well-known for its extensive ecosystem of libraries, tools, and community resources.

Keras:

• An open-source software library that offers an artificial neural network Python interface. Keras serves as the TensorFlow library's interface.

Py Torch:

• Developed by Facebook's AI Research unit, this open-source machine learning toolkit is built on the Torch library and is used for applications like computer vision and natural language processing.

XG Boost:

• An optimized distributed gradient boosting library meant to be very efficient, adaptable, and portable.

3. Prompt Engineering of AI/ML

In artificial intelligence (AI/ML), prompt engineering is the process of creating and optimizing the input prompts sent to AI models, particularly large language models (LLMs) like GPT-4, in order to obtain desired results. Prompt engineering done well may greatly enhance these models' capabilities in a variety of tasks, including as text generation, question answering, and more. Here's a thorough rundown:

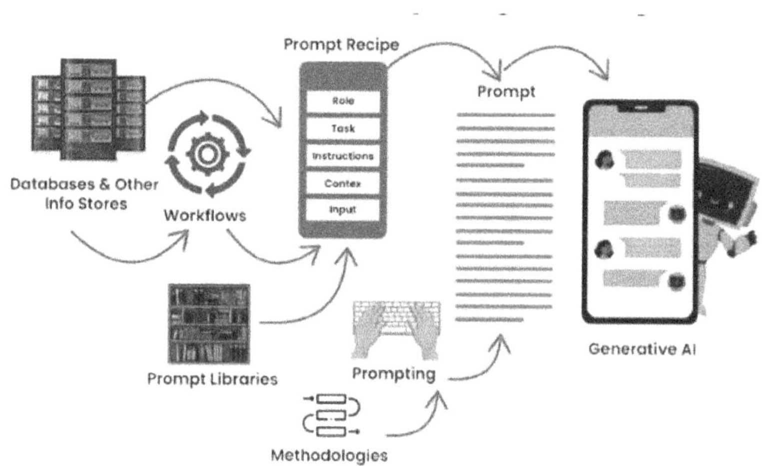

Figure. 3.1 Prompt engineering of AI/ML

Context Setting:

- Give the model the background knowledge it needs to comprehend the prompt and help it make sense of the situation.

- As an illustration, consider asking "What are the causes?" Give background information, such as "What are the causes of climate change?"

Specificity and Clarity:

- Clearly state what you want the model to do.
- For instance, ask, "Explain the fundamental concepts of quantum mechanics in simple terms," as opposed to, "Explain quantum mechanics."

Structured Prompts:

- To direct the model, use organized forms such as lists, bullet points, or detailed directions.
- For instance: "List the steps required to set up a new email account."

Role-playing:

- Give the model responsibilities to provide replies from a specific viewpoint.
- For instance: "As an experienced software developer, explain how to implement a binary search algorithm."

Example-based Prompts:

- Establish a pattern for the model to follow by giving examples.
- "Convert the following English sentences to French," as an example 1. Hi, how are you doing? 2. What time is it?"

Instruction-based Prompts:

- Give the model clear instructions on what to perform.
- For instance: "Summarize the following paragraph in one sentence."

Prompt Length and Complexity:

- Keep the prompt length in check; too long might mislead the model, and too short could lack context.
- Example: Divide the question into more manageable chunks rather than making it a big, drawn-out one.

3.1 Techniques in Prompt Engineering for Prompt engineering of AI/ML:

In AI/ML, prompt engineering approaches entail creating and optimizing prompts to maximize the output of models such as GPT-4. In the framework of AI/ML, the following comprehensive methodologies are especially designed for quick engineering:

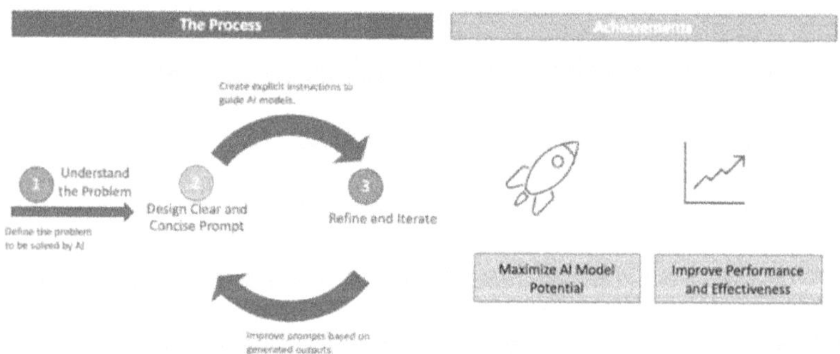

Figure. 3.2 Techniques in Prompt Engineering for Prompt engineering of AI/ML

Task Specification Prompts:

- Define the Assignment Clearly: Specify the job you want the model to complete.

- For instance: "Explain the difference between supervised and unsupervised learning."

Instructional Prompts:

- Give precise instructions: Give the model clear instructions on what to perform.

- For instance: "List the key steps involved in training a machine learning model."

Contextual Prompts:

- Provide Context: Within the prompt, provide any background information that is required.

- For instance: "In the context of natural language processing, what is the importance of tokenization?"

Example-based Prompts:

- Few-shot Learning: Give the model examples to follow.

- Example: "The following are a few instances of typical loss functions: Mean Squared Error and Cross-Entropy Loss, respectively. For what reason do loss functions become used in machine learning?

Role-specific Prompts:

- Role-playing: Give the model roles to produce replies from a specific viewpoint.

- For instance: "As a data scientist, how would you approach feature selection in a dataset with high dimensionality?"

Comparison Prompts:

- Request that the model provide comparisons and contrasts between various ideas.
- For instance: "Compare and contrast decision trees and random forests."

Step-by-Step Prompts:

- Chain of thought: Help the model to consider each stage of the process.
- Example: "Explain how machine learning uses cross-validation. Data separation should be done first."

Clarification Prompts:

- Request Clarification: Ask the model to elaborate on or provide clarification on a point.
- For instance: "Can you clarify the concept of overfitting in machine learning?"

Application Prompts:

- Ask the model to apply ideas to situations that occur in the real world.
- For instance: "How would you use a convolutional neural network for image classification?"

Applications of Artificial Intelligence and Machine Learning

Troubleshooting Prompts:

- Give the model instructions on how to troubleshoot and fix issues.
- For instance: "What are some common issues faced during model training and how can they be resolved?"

3.2 Applications of Prompt Engineering for Prompt engineering of AI/ML:

To maximize the performance of AI/ML models, prompt engineering—the process of creating efficient prompts to elicit desired outputs from the models—is essential. Within the field of AI/ML itself, rapid engineering has numerous uses, including the following:

Figure. 3.3 Applications of Prompt Engineering for Prompt engineering of AI/ML

Training Data Generation

- Creation of Synthetic Data: Machine learning models may be trained with artificial data created from prompts. When labeled data is scarce, this is very helpful.

- Augmentation: To provide more reliable model training, add variants of data points to already-existing datasets.

Model Evaluation and Testing

- Stress testing: Test the boundaries and worst-case scenarios of models using certain prompts. This aids in finding any potential biases or flaws in the models.
- Benchmarking: Create uniform questions to assess how several models perform on the same set of activities.

Fine-tuning Models

- Domain Adaptation: Create prompts that produce data or text unique to a certain domain, which can help fine-tune models for specific sectors or uses.
- Prompts Specific to Tasks: Create customized prompts to help models be optimized for certain tasks like sentiment analysis, translation, summarization, etc.

Improving Model Interpretability

- Explainability Prompts: Make prompts that produce justifications for model forecasts so that people may comprehend the reasoning behind AI choices.
- Debugging: To identify and troubleshoot problems with the model, use prompts to produce outputs.

User Interaction and Interfaces

Applications of Artificial Intelligence and Machine Learning

- Conversational AI is the design of prompts for chatbots and virtual assistants that facilitate more efficient and natural user-AI system interactions.

- Create prompts for instructional AI programs that lead students through interactive scenarios to facilitate interactive learning.

Automating Workflow and Processes

- Automation Scripts: Write instructions or scripts to automate time-consuming operations, therefore increasing data processing and analysis efficiency.

- Pipeline Integration: To build automated pipelines for data intake, preprocessing, training, and assessment, use prompts.

Creative Applications

- Content Creation: Use prompt engineering to produce artistic, musical, and narrative content.

- Design Prototyping: Create design and architectural prototypes by employing AI-generated visual and structural concepts as a guide through prompts.

Ethical AI Development

- Create prompts for the express purpose of identifying biases in AI models. This will help create more equitable and morally-responsible AI systems.

- Inclusive Training Data: Address any potential gaps in the dataset by using prompts to provide inclusive, varied training data.

Research and Development

- Hypothesis Testing: Create questions to evaluate AI/ML research ideas, which will speed up the development of fresh perspectives and methods.
- Exploratory Data Analysis: To find patterns and trends in data that might not be immediately obvious, use prompts to direct your investigation.

Customized Applications

- Customize prompts to produce recommendations or replies that are unique to each user depending on their interests or profile.
- Adaptive Systems: Create AI systems with dynamic prompt engineering that can change their behavior in response to input from users and past interactions.

Prompt engineering is a flexible and potent method that improves several areas of AI/ML, from guaranteeing inclusive and ethical development to enhancing model performance. Developers and researchers can uncover new possibilities and find creative solutions to problems by carefully constructing prompts.

3.3 Challenges and Considerations for Prompt engineering of AI/ML:

While prompt engineering has many advantages, it also has drawbacks that must be taken into account in order to optimize its performance and reduce any possible problems. The main issues and things to think about are as follows:

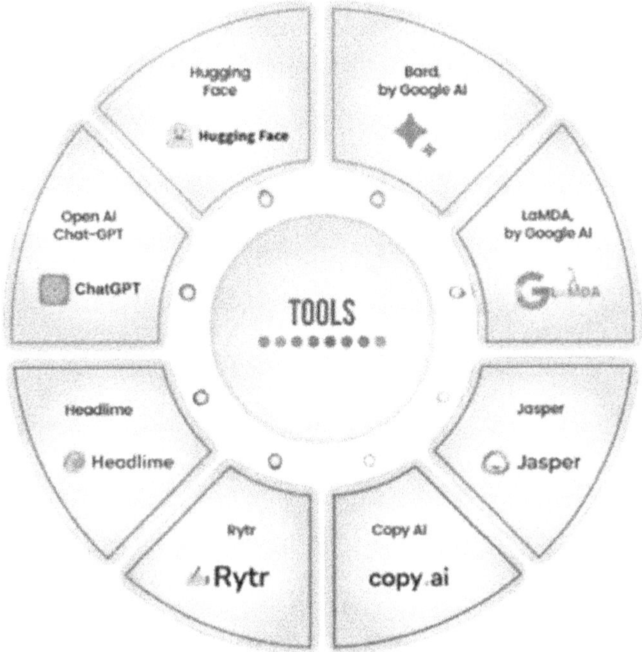

Figure. 3.4 Challenges and Considerations for Prompt engineering of AI/ML

Challenges

Ambiguity and Vagueness:

- The prompts may include too much ambiguity or vagueness, which might lead to inconsistent or irrelevant responses from the model.

- To be effective in a range of contexts, prompts need to find a balance between generality and specificity.

Bias and Fairness:

- Inadvertent reinforcement of preexisting biases in the training data by prompts may result in biased outputs.

- It might be difficult yet essential to ensure fairness and inclusion in prompt design in order to prevent discrimination and preconceptions from being reinforced.

Scalability:

- It might take a lot of effort and time to create efficient prompts for a variety of jobs and domains.
- When attempting to design prompts that are universal across several models and apps, scalability becomes a problem.

Context Dependence:

- A prompt's effectiveness might vary greatly depending on the context, so what works well in one situation might not work in another.
- It might be challenging to modify prompts for various situations without a lot of trial and error.

Complexity of Natural Language:

- Because natural language is inherently complicated and subtle, it can be difficult to design prompts that reliably result in the intended outcome.
- This complexity is increased by dealing with colloquial idioms, cultural variances, and language change.

Unintended Consequences:

- Inadequately crafted prompts may have unforeseen repercussions, including producing offensive or inaccurate text.

Applications of Artificial Intelligence and Machine Learning

- One of the main concerns is making sure that the outputs are reliable and safe.

Evaluation Metrics:

- It's difficult to create reliable measurements for assessing how effective prompts are.
- The quality and relevance of the material produced by various prompts may not be adequately measured by conventional performance measures.

Overfitting to Prompts:

- Ensuring generalization beyond specific prompt formulations is critical because models may overfit to certain prompts, yielding good results just for those prompts but failing when the prompts are modified or marginally altered.

Considerations

Clear Objective Definition:

- To inform the prompts' design, precisely state their goals and expected results.
- Gain a solid understanding of the work specifications and user expectations.

Iterative Testing and Refinement:

- Use an iterative process to create, test, and improve prompts in response to user input and performance assessments.

- Keep an eye on prompts and make necessary adjustments to increase their efficacy.

Incorporating User Feedback:

- Seek out and consider user input to make sure prompts are tailored to the requirements and preferences of the user.
- Utilize input to pinpoint problem areas and enhance prompts.

Bias Mitigation Strategies:

- Use techniques like varied training data and fairness-aware prompt design to identify and reduce bias in prompts. Conduct regular audits of prompts and outputs to check for bias and take necessary remedial action.

Context Awareness:

- When creating prompts, keep in mind the unique environment in which they will be utilized.
- When creating prompts, take into account the application domain, target audience, and cultural quirks.

Ethical Considerations:

- Respect moral standards and precepts in rapid engineering to guarantee appropriate usage of AI.
- Don't design prompts that might have negative or immoral effects.

Diversity and Inclusion:

Applications of Artificial Intelligence and Machine Learning

- Make sure the questions are inclusive and reflect a range of viewpoints and experiences.

- Steer clear of any words or situations that could be discriminatory or exclusive.

Collaboration with Domain Experts:

- Work together with subject matter experts to create prompts that are precise and pertinent to particular domains or sectors.

- Make use of domain expertise to improve the efficacy and quality of prompts.

While prompt engineering is a valuable tool for enhancing AI/ML models, it comes with a number of issues that need to be carefully considered and managed. Practitioners may maximize the benefits of rapid engineering while reducing its hazards by addressing issues with ambiguity, bias, scalability, and context dependency. They can also achieve this by following recommended practices, which include user input integration, iterative testing, and ethical concerns.

4. Effective Utilization of AI/ML

A comprehensive strategy involving many phases is required to effectively deploy AI/ML, from identifying appropriate use cases to ongoing monitoring and improvement. This is a thorough guide on using AI and ML effectively:

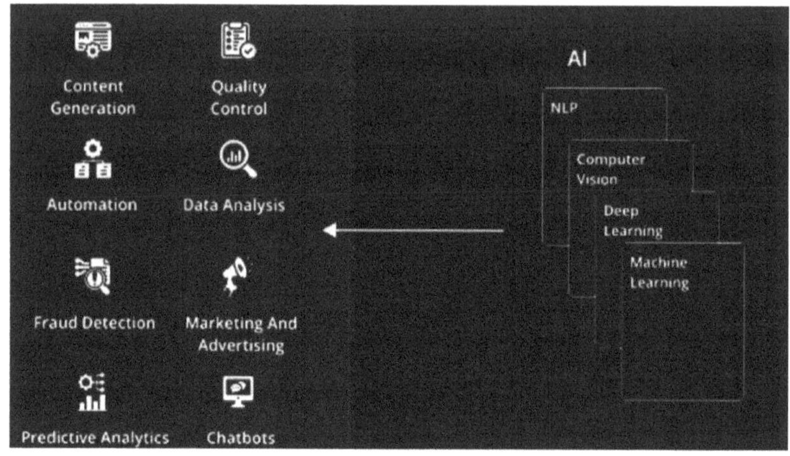

Figure.4.1 Effective utilization of AI/ML

4.1 Identify Suitable Use Cases for Effective utilization of AI/ML

The successful use of AI/ML technology depends on the identification of appropriate use cases. The following is a step-by-step methodology to assist in identifying and assessing possible AI/ML use cases:

Understand Business Objectives

Applications of Artificial Intelligence and Machine Learning Align with Strategic Goals: Determine how AI/ML may contribute to the organization's strategic goals, which may include raising revenue, enhancing customer happiness, or cutting expenses for operations.

Identify Pain Points and Opportunities

- Operational Inefficiencies: Look for procedures where automation can increase accuracy and efficiency, such as those that are labor-intensive, repetitive, or prone to human mistake.
- Data-Driven Decision Making: Determine which domains, such as market trends, consumer preferences, or risk assessment, might benefit from data analysis to get insights for improved decision-making.
- Customer Experience: Investigate how AI/ML may improve service delivery, personalize experiences, and improve customer relationships.

Assess Feasibility

- Data Availability: Make sure there is an adequate supply of high-quality data available for AI/ML model training. Lack of information can be a major obstacle.
- Technical Infrastructure: Evaluate the current technological infrastructure to determine if it can support AI/ML initiatives. Consider computational resources, storage, and integration capabilities.
- Expertise: Assess the availability of skilled personnel or the potential for upskilling existing employees to implement and maintain AI/ML solutions.

Potential Use Cases across Industries

Here are some examples of AI/ML use cases across different industries:

Healthcare

- Data Availability: Make sure there is a enough supply of high-quality data accessible for AI/ML model training. Lack of information may be a major obstacle.
- Technical Infrastructure: Assess the present state of the infrastructure to see if it is suitable for implementing AI/ML projects. Think about your storage, integration, and processing power.
- Expertise: Determine whether qualified workers are readily available or whether it is possible to upskill current staff members to develop and manage AI/ML systems.

Finance

- Fraud detection: Instantaneously recognize and stop fraudulent activity and transactions.
- Algorithmic Trading: Make trading decisions based on past performance and current market trends by utilizing AI/ML models.
- Credit scoring: Evaluate people's and companies' creditworthiness by utilizing non-traditional data sources.

Retail

Applications of Artificial Intelligence and Machine Learning

- Customer segmentation: For focused marketing, group consumers according to their past purchases, behavior, and preferences.
- Inventory management: Make use of demand predictions to optimize supply chain operations and stock levels.
- Personalized Suggestions: By making tailored product suggestions, you may improve the consumer experience.

Manufacturing

- Reduce downtime and maintenance expenses by anticipating equipment breakdowns before they happen using predictive maintenance.
- Quality Control: During the production process, use computer vision to check items for flaws.
- Supply Chain Optimization: Increase the effectiveness of the supply chain by using inventory optimization and demand forecasts.

Telecommunications

- Network Optimization: Increase network dependability and performance by using traffic control and predictive maintenance.
- Customer Churn Prediction: Spot at-risk clients and take preemptive measures to resolve their issues.
- Fraud Prevention: Track down fraudulent activity in real time, including fraudulent subscriptions and SIM switching.

Energy

- Predictive analytics is used in smart grid management to optimize energy distribution and consumption.
- Forecasting the production of electricity from renewable sources can help stabilize the grid.
- Predictive Maintenance: Track and anticipate the energy infrastructure's maintenance requirements.

Transportation and Logistics

- Route Optimization: Use AI to cut fuel costs and optimize delivery routes.
- Autonomous Vehicles: Create drones and self-driving autos for delivery and transportation.
- Demand forecasting: Estimate the need for transportation services in order to better allocate resources.

Evaluate Potential Impact

- ROI Analysis: Determine the possible return on investment by weighing the anticipated benefits against the implementation expenses.
- Scalability: Assess the AI/ML solution's capacity to expand with the company and meet new problems.
- Risk assessment: Determine and evaluate possible hazards, such as dependability of the model, data privacy, and ethical issues.

Prioritize Use Cases

- Quick Wins: To get things moving, start with initiatives that are very simple to carry out and have a good chance of succeeding.

Applications of Artificial Intelligence and Machine Learning

- Strategic Importance: Pay particular attention to use cases having the potential to have a big impact and that strongly correspond with strategic corporate goals.
- Resource Availability: When ranking use cases, take data, technology, and expertise into account.

Identifying suitable use cases for AI/ML requires a thorough understanding of business objectives, pain points, data availability, and technical feasibility. By carefully evaluating these factors and prioritizing use cases based on potential impact and strategic importance, organizations can effectively harness the power of AI/ML to drive innovation and achieve business goals.

4.2 Data Management for Effective utilization of AI/ML

Successful data management is essential for AI/ML projects to succeed. Data handling best practices guarantee that models are trained on representative, pertinent, and high-quality datasets, which has a direct impact on the models' dependability and performance. This is a thorough approach on data management for using AI and ML effectively:

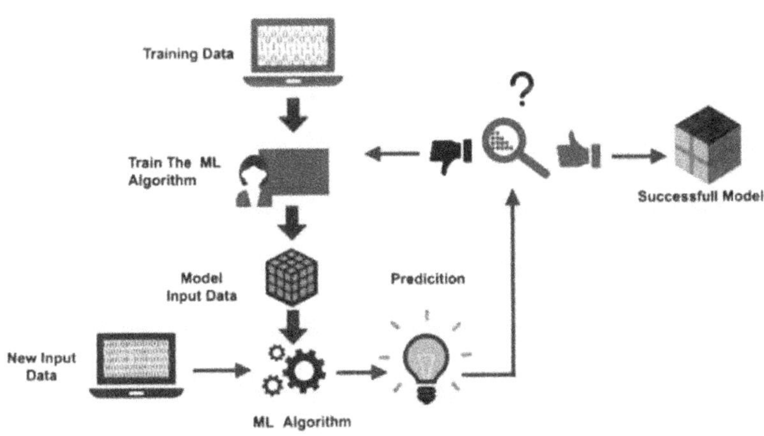

Figure.4.2 Data Management for Effective utilization of AI/ML

Data Collection

Sources

- Internal Data: Gather information from logs, sensors, transaction databases, CRM, and ERP, among other internal systems.

- External Data: Add to internal data from sources such as web scraping, public databases, social media, and third-party data providers.

- Real-time Data: Make use of online transactions, streaming data from Internet of Things devices, and real-time user interactions.

Methods

- APIs: To integrate and gather data from several sources, use APIs.

- Manual Entry: In order to minimize human mistake, manual entry should be limited to smaller datasets where it may be practical.

- Automated Data collecting: To automate data collecting procedures, use tools and scripts.

Data Cleaning

Handling Missing Data

- Imputation: Use the mean, median, mode, or more advanced techniques like regression or K-nearest neighbors (KNN) to fill in the missing data.

- Removal: If a row or column has a large percentage of missing values and is not important, remove it.

Error Correction

- Check for inconsistencies in data submissions by identifying and fixing things like various date formats or measurement units.
- Outlier Identification: Use statistical techniques or domain-specific guidelines to identify and manage outliers.

De-duplication

- Duplicate Detection: To maintain data integrity, find duplicate records and combine them.

Data Annotation and Labeling

Labeling Data

- Labeling data can be done in three ways: manually by using human annotators (especially for tasks like entity recognition, image recognition, and sentiment analysis);
- Through crowdsourcing (using sites like Amazon Mechanical Turk for large-scale annotation tasks);
- Automatically (using semi-supervised or unsupervised methods where practical).

Quality Assurance

- Verification: Put procedures in place to ensure that labeled data is accurate and consistent.

- Inter-annotator Agreement: To preserve label quality, assess and guarantee strong agreement between various annotators.

Data Storage and Management

Storage Solutions

- Cloud storage: Use cloud services (AWS, Google Cloud, and Azure) for scalable and flexible storage solutions.
- Databases: Depending on the data type and requirements, use relational (SQL) or non-relational (NoSQL) databases.
- Data lakes: Store large volumes of raw data in a centralized repository for future processing and analysis.

Data Governance

- Data Policies: Define guidelines for the security, exchange, and access to data.
- Compliance: Make sure that industry-specific guidelines and data protection laws like the CCPA and GDPR are followed.
- Data Lineage: Monitor the beginning, traveling, and changing of data over the course of its existence.

Data Preprocessing

Normalization and Scaling

- Normalization: To guarantee consistency between features, scale data to a common range, usually [0, 1] or [-1, 1].

- Standardization: Convert data to a mean of 0 and a standard deviation of 1, which is helpful for logistic regression and support vector machines (SVM) methods.

Feature Engineering

- Feature Selection: To enhance model performance, determine and pick the most essential characteristics.
- Feature Creation: To better capture underlying patterns in the data, create new features from the existing data.

Data Augmentation

Techniques

- Image Data: To improve dataset variety, use modifications including rotation, flipping, cropping, and color correction.
- Text Data: To generate variants, use back-translation, random insertion, and synonym substitution.
- Synthetic Data: Create synthetic data for unbalanced datasets by applying techniques such as SMOTE (Synthetic Minority Over-sampling Technique) or GANs (Generative Adversarial Networks).

Data Splitting

Training, Validation, and Test Sets

- Training Set: Train the model using most of the data.
- Validation Set: For model selection and hyper parameter adjustment, use a different set.

- Test Set: To assess the model's performance, use a last hold-out set.

Cross-Validation

- K-Fold Cross-Validation: Divide the data into k subgroups. Rotate through all of the subsets while training on k-1 subsets.

Continuous Data Management

Data Monitoring

- Data Drift Detection: Keep an eye out for distributional shifts in the data that might have an impact on model performance.
- Control the quality of the data by conducting routine inspections to keep it that way throughout time.

Updating Data

- Update datasets incrementally to include new information and emerging patterns.
- Retraining Models: To keep models accurate and relevant, retrain them on current data on a regular basis.

The successful implementation of AI/ML models requires effective data management. It entails a thorough method of gathering, sanitizing, storing, preprocessing, augmenting, and managing data continuously. Organizations may greatly improve the effectiveness and dependability of their AI/ML systems by making sure that their data is of the highest caliber, correctly preserved, and arranged.

4.3 Model Selection and Development for Effective utilization of AI/ML

The AI/ML lifecycle's crucial stages of model creation and selection determine the dependability and efficacy of the implemented solution. This entails selecting the appropriate algorithms, maximizing their effectiveness, and making sure they are appropriate for the particular issue at hand. This is a comprehensive reference on model building and selection for efficient AI/ML use:

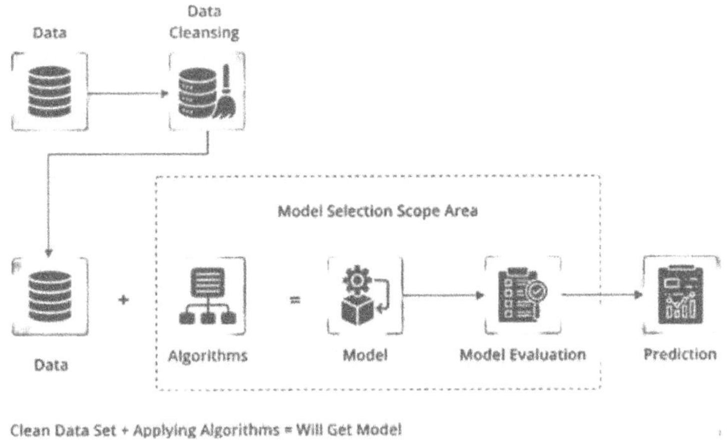

Figure.4.3 Model Selection and Development for Effective utilization of AI/ML

Understand the Problem and Data

Problem Definition

- Determine the problem's kind by determining if it involves reinforcement learning, regression, classification, or clustering.

- Establish precise goals and performance indicators for the model.

Data Characteristics

- Data Type: Recognize the type of data (text, picture, structured, unstructured, etc.).
- Analyze the volume and caliber of the data that are now accessible.

Exploratory Data Analysis (EDA)

- To comprehend the distributions, correlations, and patterns of the data, do EDA.
- Plots such as histograms, scatter plots, box plots, etc. can be used to visualize data.
- Determine and deal with abnormalities and outliers.

Feature Engineering

- To improve model performance, create additional features from the data that already exists.
- Using methods such as feature importance ratings, correlation analysis, etc., choose the most pertinent characteristics.
- If required, reduce the dimensionality using techniques such as Principal Component Analysis (PCA).

Model Selection

Choose the Appropriate Algorithm

- For supervised learning:

Applications of Artificial Intelligence and Machine Learning

- Classification: Support vector machines (SVM), Decision trees, random forests, neural networks, logistic regression, etc.
- Regression: Decision trees, random forests, neural networks, Ridge/Lasso regression, linear regression, etc.
- For unsupervised learning:
  - Clustering techniques: DBSCAN, K-Means, Hierarchical Clustering, etc.
  - Reducing Dimensionality: PCA, t-SNE, etc.

Baseline Models

Establish a foundation for performance by starting with basic models.

Model Comparison

- Utilize cross-validation to assess several models.
- Analyze performance indicators including regression's RMSE and MAE and classification's F1 score, recall, accuracy, and precision.

Model Training and hyper parameter tuning

Training Models

- Utilizing the training dataset, train many models.
- Employ suitable optimization methods and loss functions.

Hyper parameter Tuning

- Use methods such as Grid Search, Random Search, or Bayesian Optimization to do hyper parameter tweaking.
- Tuning should be guided by validation set performance.

SANTOSH REDDY ADDULA, R. DURGA MEENA, E.GEETHA RANI, D. ANUSHA

- Use methods such as Grid Search, Random Search, or Bayesian Optimization to do hyper parameter tweaking.
- Tuning should be guided by validation set performance.

5. Control Points of AI/ML

The term "control points" in AI/ML (Artificial Intelligence/Machine Intelligence) refers to critical domains where regulation, supervision, and control are required to guarantee the ethical, safe, and advantageous application of AI technology. These safety measures can guarantee compliance with human values, reduce dangers, and stop abuse. The following are some crucial checkpoints:

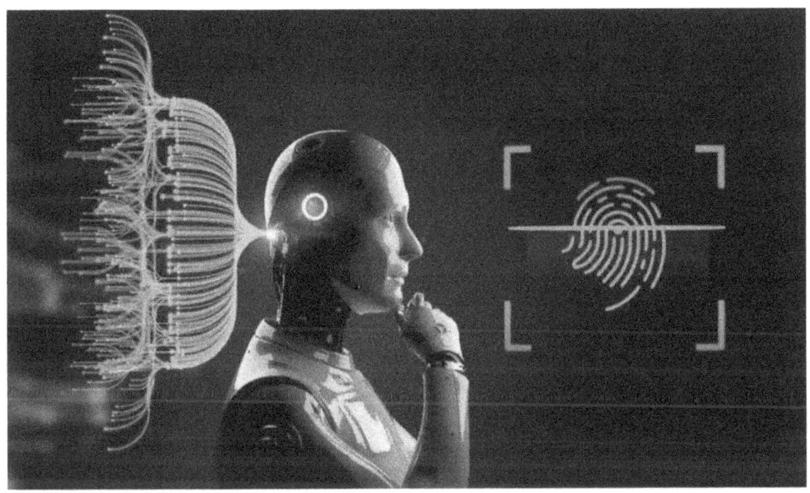

Figure.5.1 Control Points of AI/ML

5.1 Data Governance for Control Points of AI/ML

The process of developing frameworks and policies for data governance for AI/ML (Artificial Intelligence/Machine Intelligence) control points entails making sure that the data used in AI systems is managed safely, ethically, and effectively throughout its lifespan. The main elements of data governance for AI/ML control points are as follows:

Data Quality and Integrity

- Accuracy: Make sure the data is error-free and accurate. When gathering and preparing data, make sure validity checks are implemented.

- Completeness: Make sure datasets contain all relevant data and are thorough. Find and fix any holes or information that is missing.

- Consistency: To guarantee compatibility, keep consistent data formats and standards across various datasets.

- Timeliness: Make sure the information is current and pertinent. Establish procedures for timely data collection and frequent updates.

- Provenance: To verify the reliability of data, track its origin and history, including any alterations it may have undergone.

Data Privacy

- Anonymization and De-identification: To preserve individual privacy, remove or obfuscate personal identifiers from data.

- Managing user consent for the gathering, use, and sharing of data is known as consent management. Make sure data procedures are transparent.

- Role-based access restrictions should be used to limit authorized personnel's access to data.

Applications of Artificial Intelligence and Machine Learning

- Respect for Privacy Laws: Make sure that data protection laws, including the CCPA, GDPR, and others that are pertinent to the area, are followed.

Data Security

- Encryption: To prevent unwanted access and security breaches, encrypt data both in transit and at rest.
- Install intrusion detection systems (IDS) to keep an eye out for unwanted access and unusual data consumption.
- Frequent Security Audits: To detect and mitigate possible threats, do frequent security audits and vulnerability assessments.
- Plans for handling issues: Create and update incident response plans to quickly handle security issues and data breaches.

Data Management

- Data Storage: Put in place scalable, resilient, and safe data storage options that are capable of handling substantial data volumes.
- Data Retention Policies: Clearly define the duration of data retention as well as the steps involved in deleting data when it is no longer required.
- Data Backup and Recovery: To avoid data loss, make sure to regularly do backups and have solid procedures for data recovery.
- Data cataloging: To make it easier to find, retrieve, and utilize data, keep an extensive catalog of datasets.

Data Lifecycle Management

- Establish guidelines for the moral and legal gathering of data while making sure that all applicable laws are followed.
- Data Preparation and Cleaning: Create uniform procedures for cleaning, normalization, and transformation as part of data pretreatment.
- Data Annotation and Labeling: Make sure that the data used to train AI models is accurately and consistently labeled.
- Guidelines for safe and moral data sharing with outside partners and collaborators should be established.

Data Ethics and Compliance

- The development and implementation of ethical guidelines for data usage is vital to ensure that it is in accordance with societal norms and values.
- Fairness and Bias: Take steps to identify and reduce data biases that may provide biased or unjust AI results.
- Accountability and Transparency: Make sure that data governance procedures are transparent, and set up accountability systems for data handling procedures.

Data Monitoring and Auditing

- Constant Monitoring: To guarantee adherence to governance guidelines, put in place mechanisms for continuing to keep an eye on how data is being used.

Applications of Artificial Intelligence and Machine Learning

- Frequent Audits: Review data governance procedures on a frequent basis to find weaknesses and make necessary adjustments.
- Performance Metrics: To evaluate the efficacy of data governance methods, identify and monitor key performance indicators (KPIs).

Stakeholder Engagement and Training

- Training Courses: Provide courses on data governance, security, and privacy for staff members.
- Involve stakeholders in the creation and evaluation of data governance policies, including data subjects.
- Feedback Systems: Set up systems to collect opinions from interested parties and keep refining data governance procedures.

Implementation Steps:

- Create a Governance Framework: Create a thorough framework for data governance that includes guidelines for standards, practices, and policies.
- Assign Responsibilities: Establish roles and duties for the governance of data, including the designation of governance committees and data stewards.
- Create guidelines and protocols: Make thorough guidelines and protocols for every aspect of data governance.
- Put Technology Solutions into Practice: Make use of technology solutions for monitoring, auditing, data management, and security.

- Continuous Improvement: Evaluate and improve data governance procedures on a regular basis in response to audit findings, user feedback, and changing legal requirements.

5.2 Algorithm Transparency and Explain ability for Control Points of AI/ML

Algorithm transparency and explain ability are crucial control points in AI/ML (Artificial Intelligence/Machine Intelligence), ensuring that AI systems' decision-making processes are clear and understandable to users, stakeholders, and regulators. These control points help build trust, enable accountability, and facilitate compliance with ethical and legal standards. Here are the key components and implementation strategies for achieving algorithm transparency and explain ability:

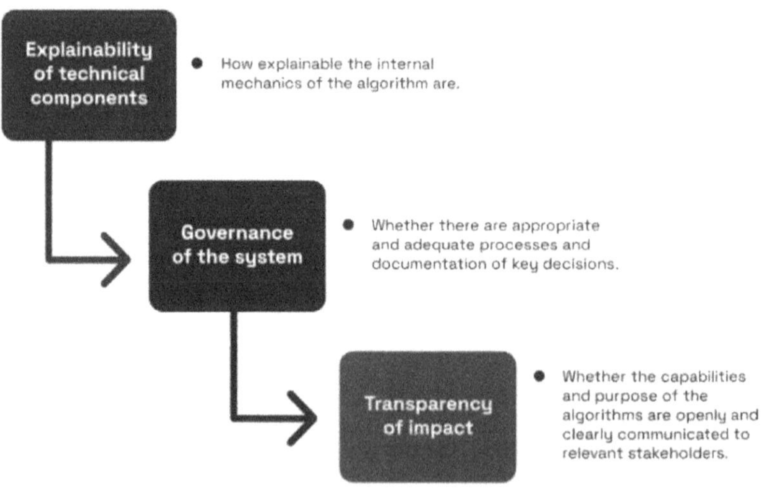

Figure.5.2 Algorithm Transparency and Explain ability for Control Points of AI/ML

Applications of Artificial Intelligence and Machine Learning

Transparency

- Provide thorough documentation of the AI models, outlining their constraints, design decisions, and organizational framework.
- Provide information about the kinds and sources of data that are used for operations and training. Describe feature engineering and data pretreatment in detail.
- Algorithmic Transparency: Educate stakeholders on the algorithms and how they work. This includes making the model's design and training procedure public.

Explainability

- User-Friendly Explanations: Create explanations that laypeople with little experience can grasp. Explain to us how the AI makes decisions in simple words.
- The significance of features Determine and convey the elements or inputs that have the greatest influence during the decision-making process.
- Decision Pathways: Describe the sequential steps used by the AI system to reach a specific choice or result.

Implementation Strategies

Design for Explainability

- Model Selection: Whenever feasible, choose interpretable models such as rule-based systems, decision trees, or linear models.

- Post-Hoc Explanations: To explain complex models, use methods like SHAP (Shapley Additive explanations) or LIME (Local Interpretable Model-agnostic Explanations).
- Model-Neutral Approaches: To ensure broad application, use methods that offer explanations independent of the underlying model.

Stakeholder Engagement

- Interactive Interfaces: Provide user interfaces that let interested parties engage with the AI system and investigate the decision-making process.
- Feedback Mechanisms: Gather user input and apply it to improve and hone explanations.
- Transparency Reports: Publish reports on a regular basis that explain the goals, functionality, and decision-making procedures of the AI system.

Regulatory and Ethical Compliance

- Respect for Guidelines: Comply with established standards and guidelines, such as those from IEEE, ISO, and other regulatory authorities, for AI transparency and explainability.
- Conduct routine compliance audits to make sure that the rules pertaining to explainability and openness are being followed.

Tools and Techniques

Applications of Artificial Intelligence and Machine Learning

- Tools for Explainable AI (XAI): Make use of specific frameworks and tools intended to improve the explainability of AI models.
- Illustrations: Make use of visual aids like as flow diagrams, charts, and graphs to illustrate decision-making procedures and feature significance.

Education and Training

- Training Programs: Create educational programs to help users, developers, and other stakeholders comprehend the explainability and transparency of AI.
- Create tutorials, guidelines, and other educational materials to assist stakeholders in understanding AI principles and explanations.

5.3 Ethical and Fair Use for Control Points of AI/ML

Making sure AI systems are created and applied in ways that are just, equitable, and consistent with society values is a key component of the ethical and fair use of AI/ML (Artificial Intelligence/Machine Intelligence). This calls for resolving any biases, guaranteeing equity, and upholding moral standards all the way through the AI lifetime. The following are the main elements and tactics for encouraging a just and moral application of AI/ML:

Ethical and Fair Use

Bias Mitigation

- Bias Identification: To find and comprehend potential biases, check datasets and algorithms on a regular basis.

- Reducing or eliminating biases in data and models can be accomplished by applying strategies like resampling, reweighting, or applying fairness requirements during model training.

Fairness

- Fair Treatment: Make sure AI systems handle people and groups equally, without prejudice against them on the basis of their age, gender, race, or any other protected characteristic.
- Equitable Access: Make an effort to give people from all backgrounds and geographical areas equal access to the advantages of AI technologies.

Ethical Guidelines

- Ethical Frameworks: Create and follow moral standards guiding AI system design, implementation, and use.
- Align AI systems with human values and social standards to promote wellbeing and prevent damage. This is known as value alignment.

Accountability

- Assigning Responsibilities: Clearly state who inside the company is responsible for what decisions and activities involving AI.
- Transparent Reporting: Ensure that AI decisions and activities are transparent, giving stakeholder's easily understandable justifications.

Applications of Artificial Intelligence and Machine Learning
Privacy and Consent

- Data privacy: Put strong safeguards in place to guard sensitive and private information used by AI systems.
- Make sure people give their informed consent before any data is collected or judgments made using AI that may have an impact on them.

Implementation Strategies

Inclusive Design

- Diverse Teams: To bring a variety of viewpoints and lower the possibility of bias, put together diverse development teams.
- Involve a variety of stakeholders, including underrepresented groups, in the development and application of AI systems.

Ethical Audits

- Conduct Ethics Audits on a Regular Basis: Evaluate AI systems on an ongoing basis to make sure they meet fairness standards and ethical principles.
- Independent Review: Have impartial outsiders examine and vouch for the moral rectitude of AI systems.

Training and Awareness

- Ethics Education: Educate developers, data scientists, and other interested parties on moral standards and just procedures in artificial intelligence.

- Campaigns for Awareness: Educate users and the general public about the ethical implications of AI technologies by organizing awareness campaigns.

Bias Detection and Mitigation Tools

- Fairness Toolkits: To identify and reduce bias in AI models, make use of toolkits such as Google's What-If Tool or IBM's AI Fairness 360.
- Continuous Monitoring: Put in place mechanisms for tracking and correcting biases as they appear.

Legal and Regulatory Compliance

- Respect for Laws: Make sure AI systems abide by pertinent laws and rules pertaining to consumer rights, data protection, and discrimination.
- Ethical Guidelines: Adhere to the guidelines and best practices established by trade associations and other industry groups.

5.4 Safety and Reliability for Control Points of AI/ML

For the development and implementation of AI/ML (Artificial Intelligence/Machine Intelligence) systems, safety and dependability are essential control points. Building confidence, preventing harm, and ensuring AI systems function as intended under a variety of circumstances and over an extended period of time are all facilitated by ensuring their safe and dependable operation. The following are the essential elements and tactics for advancing security and dependability in AI/ML:

Safety and Reliability

Robustness

- Adversarial Robustness: Make sure AI systems are resilient to attacks intended to trick or control them.

- Ensure environmental robustness by ensuring AI systems operate dependably in a variety of situations and environmental settings.

Validation and Verification

- Model Validation: To make sure AI models satisfy performance and safety requirements, test and validate them methodically.

- Verification Procedures: Put formal verification procedures in place to demonstrate mathematically that AI systems function as intended.

Redundancy and Fault Tolerance

- Redundant Systems: To ensure operation in the event of a breakdown, design AI systems with redundant components.

- Make that AI systems are capable of identifying and resolving mistakes and defects without suffering from appreciable performance reduction.

Monitoring and Maintenance

- Constant Monitoring: Use real-time tracking to identify irregularities, mistakes, or problems with performance.

- Frequent Maintenance: To fix problems, vulnerabilities, and changing needs, do routine maintenance and updates.

Safety Protocols

- Create fail-safe procedures to guarantee that, in the event of a failure, AI systems revert to a safe state.
- Establish emergency shutdown protocols that can be triggered in the event that an unforeseen behavior by the AI system occurs.

Implementation Strategies

Risk Assessment and Management

- Risk Identification: Determine the possible dangers and ways in which AI systems can fail.
- Plans for mitigating identified risks should be created and put into action. These plans should include backup plans in case of major malfunctions.

Testing and Evaluation

- Stress testing: To assess how AI systems function under demanding circumstances or loads, conduct stress tests.
- Before deploying AI systems in the real world, use simulations to simulate and forecast their behavior in a variety of scenarios.

Standards and Best Practices

Applications of Artificial Intelligence and Machine Learning

- Adherence to Standards: For AI safety and dependability, abide by industry standards and best practices, such as those provided by NIST or ISO/IEC.
- Benchmarking: Evaluate AI systems on a regular basis using accepted safety and dependability parameters.

Human Oversight

- Human-in-the-Loop: Make sure that crucial decision-making processes have human monitoring in order to identify and fix mistakes.
- Establish transparent accountability frameworks for faults and failures of AI systems.

Transparency and Documentation

- Thorough Documentation: Keep thorough records of the processes involved in the design, testing, and upkeep of AI systems.
- Transparency Reports: Disseminate transparency reports outlining the efficaciousness of the safety and dependability measures in place.

5.5 Human Oversight and Control for Control Points of AI/ML

To guarantee that AI/ML (Artificial Intelligence/Machine Intelligence) systems are secure, moral, and consistent with human values, human oversight and control are necessary at vital points. Here are some important things to think about:

Design and Development

- Human-in-the-loop (HITL) systems include people in the AI's decision-making process and provide them the ability to change or override choices.

- Transparent Design: Make sure AI systems are transparently constructed, with decision-making procedures well documented.

- Bias Mitigation: Put techniques in place to find and lessen biases in AI systems, guaranteeing equity and justice.

Deployment and Monitoring

- Continuous Monitoring: Make sure AI systems are continuously monitored in order to spot anomalies, mistakes, or departures from normal behavior.

- Feedback Loops: Establish channels for user input to continuously enhance the functionality of the AI system and resolve any problems.

- Auditing and Compliance: Make sure AI systems are routinely audited to make sure they adhere to industry best practices, regulatory requirements, and ethical standards.

Decision-Making and Action

- Explainability and Transparency: Make sure people can clearly understand the reasoning behind AI decisions and the actions they conduct.

- Accountability Frameworks: Clearly outline who is in charge of what results and establish accountability frameworks for AI decisions.

- Human Override Capability: When necessary, design systems such that human operators may step in and take over AI choices.

Ethical and Legal Considerations

- Ethical rules: Create and abide by ethical rules that cover issues such as permission, privacy, and the effect on employment while using AI.
- Legal Compliance: Verify that AI systems abide by all applicable laws and rules, including those pertaining to data protection and industry-specific guidelines.
- Impact Assessment: To analyze the societal and ethical ramifications of AI systems, conduct impact assessments on a regular basis.

Training and Education

- User Education: Give users and operators of AI systems thorough instruction so they can comprehend the capabilities, constraints, and control mechanisms of these systems.
- Public Awareness: Raise public knowledge of AI technology, including their possible effects on society.
- Professional Development: To keep up with the most recent developments and ethical norms, AI developers and practitioners should be encouraged to pursue continual professional development.

Collaborative Governance

- Involve a wide range of stakeholders in the governance of AI systems, such as industry professionals, decision-makers, and members of the public.

- Multidisciplinary Methods: Utilize knowledge from a variety of fields, including the social sciences, law, and ethics, to guide the creation and regulation of artificial intelligence.

- Worldwide Cooperation: Promote worldwide cooperation to unify standards and laws and to meet the global challenges brought by artificial intelligence.

5.6 Regulation and Compliance for Control Points of AI/ML

To address ethical, legal, and safety problems, it is imperative to regulate and ensure compliance for AI/ML (Artificial Intelligence/Machine Intelligence) control points. The following are crucial areas and tactics for efficient regulation and adherence:

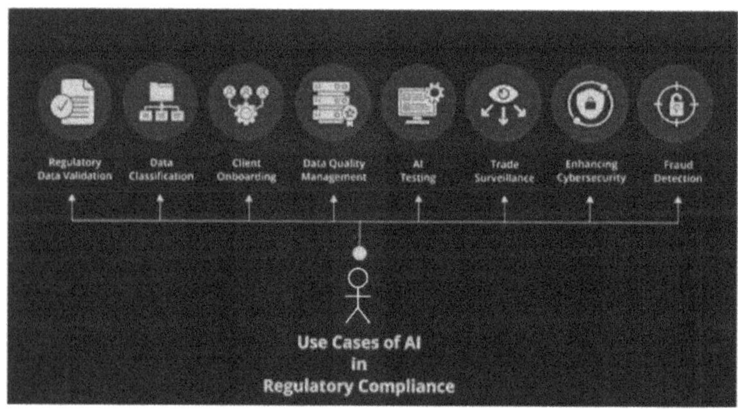

Figure.5.3 Regulation and Compliance for Control Points of AI/ML

Applications of Artificial Intelligence and Machine Learning
Establishing Regulatory Frameworks

- Enact comprehensive legislation: Create rules and laws that particularly handle the special difficulties and dangers posed by AI technologies.
- Rules and Recommendations: Establish industry norms and regulations for the creation, implementation, and oversight of AI systems.
- Ethical Codes: Encourage the adoption of moral guidelines that prioritize values such as accountability, transparency, and fairness for both AI developers and users.

Data Protection and Privacy

- Data Governance: Put in place strong data governance guidelines to guarantee that data utilized by AI systems is collected, used, and shared responsibly.
- Privacy Regulations: Adhere to the rules governing data privacy, such as the General Data Protection Regulation (GDPR) in Europe, which specify the handling of personal data.
- Consent Mechanisms: Make certain that people whose data is being utilized provide clear, informed consent to AI systems.

Bias and Fairness

- Conduct routine audits to identify and address biases in datasets and AI systems.
- Develop and implement fairness measures to assess how AI systems affect various demographic groups.

- Promote inclusive design methods that incorporate a range of viewpoints into the creation of AI.

Transparency and Explainability

- Algorithmic Transparency: Demand that pertinent stakeholders be informed of AI algorithms and decision-making procedures.
- Create AI systems that can give comprehensible justifications for the choices and behaviors they make. This is known as explainable AI.
- Documentation and Reporting: To promote accountability and transparency, keep thorough records of documentation and reporting procedures for AI systems.

Safety and Security

- Robust Testing: Before deploying AI systems, make sure they are safe and reliable by putting them through stringent testing procedures.
- Security Measures: To shield AI systems from malevolent attacks and unlawful access, implement cutting-edge cybersecurity measures.
- Build AI systems with fail-safe features to reduce or eliminate damage in the event that a system malfunctions.

Accountability and Liability

- Clear Accountability Structures: Identify and designate particular people or groups as responsible for AI choices and results.

Applications of Artificial Intelligence and Machine Learning

- Establish liability frameworks to handle injury or damage brought about by AI systems, making sure that those who cause it are held liable.
- Establish independent organizations or agencies to keep an eye on adherence to AI laws and guidelines.

Continuous Monitoring and Auditing

- Real-Time Monitoring: To continuously monitor the behavior and performance of AI systems, put in place real-time monitoring systems.
- Periodic Audits: To guarantee continuous adherence to legal obligations and moral standards, conduct audits and evaluations on a regular basis.
- Feedback and Improvement: Establish processes for ongoing feedback and enhancement so that AI systems can be updated and modified on schedule.

International Coordination and Harmonization

- Global Standards: To guarantee uniformity and prevent regulatory arbitrage, work toward the unification of AI laws and standards across many nations and areas.
- International Cooperation: Encourage cross-border cooperation and coordination on AI regulation, exchanging best practices and working together to tackle global issues.
- Cross-Border Data Flows: Create mechanisms to oversee cross-border data transfers and guarantee adherence to global data security regulations.

Stakeholder Engagement and Public Participation

- Inclusive Policymaking: Involve a broad spectrum of stakeholders in the policy-making process for artificial intelligence, such as the public, civil society, and industry experts.
- Campaigns for Public Awareness: Run public awareness efforts to inform people about the rights they have under AI rules and the ramifications of AI.
- Consultative Procedures: Provide mechanisms for public comment and input on laws and policies pertaining to artificial intelligence.

Adaptability and Responsiveness

- Dynamic Regulation: Create flexible legal frameworks that can react to new threats and the quick development of AI technology.
- Regulatory Sandboxes: Before broader adoption, evaluate novel AI technologies and regulatory strategies in a controlled setting using regulatory sandboxes.
- Ongoing study: In order to guide future regulatory changes, support ongoing study into the moral, legal, and social consequences of artificial intelligence.

5.7 Monitoring and Auditing for Control Points of AI/ML

For AI/ML systems to comply with operational, regulatory, and ethical norms, monitoring and auditing are essential. The following are essential tactics and approaches for efficiently keeping an eye on and auditing AI/ML control points:

Applications of Artificial Intelligence and Machine Learning
Continuous Monitoring

- Real-Time Data Analysis: Use real-time data analysis tools to track the performance of AI systems over time and identify anomalies and departures from typical behavior.
- Performance measures: To gauge the efficacy, efficiency, and security of AI systems, establish and monitor key performance measures (KPIs).
- Automated Alerts: Configure automated alerts to inform relevant parties of any anomalous behavior or possible problems with the AI system.

Regular Audits

- Internal Audits: Perform routine internal audits to check that AI systems are designed, implemented, and operated in accordance with organizational standards and regulations.
- External Audits: Hire outside auditors to independently evaluate AI systems and confirm that they adhere to legal and industry norms.
- Algorithm audits: In particular, audit the algorithms that AI systems employ to find biases, guarantee justice, and verify accuracy.

Bias and Fairness Assessments

- Tools for Bias Detection: To identify and quantify biases in AI models and datasets, use specialist tools.

- Fairness audits: Conduct regular audits of AI systems to see how they affect various demographic groups and guarantee fair treatment.
- Corrective Actions: Take action to rectify any biases or difficulties with fairness that are found during audits.

Security and Privacy Audits

- Conduct security audits to find weaknesses and make sure that strong cybersecurity safeguards are in place.
- Privacy Impact Assessments: To review how AI systems manage personal data and guarantee compliance with data protection rules, conduct privacy impact assessments, or PIAs.
- Data handling audits: Examine data handling procedures to make sure that information is gathered, saved, and handled morally and securely.

Explainability and Transparency

- Tools for Explainability: Apply strategies and instruments that improve AI systems' explainability, bringing transparency to their decision-making procedures.
- Review of Documentation: To make sure AI systems have clear documentation and transparent operations, review documentation on a regular basis.
- User input: Gather and examine user input to learn more about how people view AI judgments and to increase transparency.

Ethical Compliance

Applications of Artificial Intelligence and Machine Learning

- Conduct audits to verify that AI systems adhere to moral principles and standards.
- Committees on Ethics: Create committees on ethics to supervise the creation and application of AI systems and guarantee that moral standards are followed.
- Impact Assessments: To analyze the societal and ethical ramifications of AI systems, conduct impact assessments on a regular basis.

Accountability and Governance

- Establish governance frameworks that specify the obligations, responsibilities, and lines of accountability for AI systems.
- Audit Trails: To ensure accountability, keep thorough audit trails that record all decisions and activities taken by AI systems.
- Compliance Reporting: Prepare periodic compliance reports that include an overview of audit results as well as the state of standards and regulation compliance.

Training and Awareness

- Employee Education: Educate employees on best practices for auditing and monitoring systems to make sure they have the abilities to manage AI systems with efficiency.
- Awareness Campaigns: To inform interested parties about the significance of keeping an eye on and auditing AI systems, run awareness campaigns.

- Encourage professional development and ongoing education in the areas of AI ethics, regulation, and auditing.

Adaptive Monitoring Systems

- Dynamic Monitoring Tools: Provide flexible monitoring systems that can change as the AI system does, taking into account new features and potential threats.
- Establish feedback loops that allow AI systems to be continuously improved based on audit and monitoring results.
- Scenario Analysis: To foresee and get ready for possible problems with AI systems, use scenario analysis and stress testing.

Stakeholder Engagement

- User Participation: Obtain feedback and viewpoints from users and other stakeholders by involving them in the monitoring and auditing process.
- Collaborative Audits: Share best practices and insights when conducting collaborative audits with regulators, industry partners, and other stakeholders.
- Public Transparency: Increase public trust in AI systems by disclosing audit results and monitoring reports.

5.8 User Education and Awareness for Control Points of AI/ML

To ensure that AI/ML (Artificial Intelligence/Machine Intelligence) technologies are used ethically and successfully, user awareness and education are crucial. The following tactics

Applications of Artificial Intelligence and Machine Learning and methods aim to improve user awareness and education regarding AI/ML control points:

Educational Programs and Resources

- Workshops and Training Sessions: To inform users about the capabilities and constraints of AI/ML systems, arrange workshops and training sessions.
- Online Courses: Provide a range of topics related to artificial intelligence, such as safety, ethics, and real-world applications.
- User manuals and guides: Provide thorough instructions on how to communicate with and manage artificial intelligence (AI) systems via user manuals and guides.

Awareness Campaigns

- Public Awareness Campaigns: Start initiatives to increase public knowledge of the possible advantages and disadvantages of artificial intelligence.
- Social Media and Online Platforms: Make use of these channels to interact with the public and spread knowledge about AI-related issues.
- Partnerships with Academic Institutions: Work together with colleges, universities, and schools to include AI education into their curricula.

Interactive Learning Tools

- Simulations and Interactive Demonstrations: Produce simulations and interactive demonstrations that let consumers observe and comprehend the behavior of artificial intelligence.

- Create gamified learning opportunities to make AI education interesting and approachable.

- Virtual Assistants: Give consumers real-time information and direction on utilizing AI technology by utilizing virtual assistants.

Transparency and Explainability

- Use explainable AI (XAI) techniques to make sure people comprehend the decision-making process of AI systems.

- Transparency Reports: Disseminate reports that provide information on the impact, decision-making procedures, and operation of AI systems.

- Clear Communication: When communicating technical details, use language that is both understandable and clear; stay away from jargon and complicated terminology.

Ethics and Responsibility

- Ethics Education: Stress the value of responsible AI use and the moral ramifications of AI judgments in your ethics education sessions for users.

- Case Studies: Use case studies to highlight moral conundrums and the best ways to use AI.

- User Responsibilities: Inform users of their rights to data privacy and informed consent when working with AI systems.

Feedback and Engagement

Applications of Artificial Intelligence and Machine Learning

- Establish channels for users to offer input on AI systems, which will aid in identifying problems and potential areas for development.

- Community Forums: Establish community forums where users can exchange expertise, talk about their experiences, and pose inquiries regarding artificial intelligence.

- Involve a wide variety of stakeholders in conversations around the creation and application of AI.

Regulatory and Legal Awareness

- Legal Compliance Training: Inform users about the laws and rules that apply to AI, including those pertaining to privacy and data protection.

- Users should be made aware of their legal rights and safeguards with regard to artificial intelligence.

- Updates on Regulations: Inform users of any changes to legislation and how they may affect the use of AI.

Personalized Learning

- Tailored Training Plans: Create training plans specifically for various user groups, including managers, end users, and technical personnel.

- Use adaptive learning platforms: These platforms adapt the information to the user's level of expertise and learning speed.

- One-on-One mentorship: To assist users in comprehending and using AI systems efficiently, provide one-on-one mentorship and support.

Collaborations and Partnerships

- Industry Partnerships: Work together with top players in the field to give users access to the most recent information and AI best practices.
- Government Initiatives: Collaborate with government organizations to run public programs that increase public knowledge about and literacy about AI.
- Nonprofit Organizations: Collaborate with nonprofit organizations to spread the word about ethical AI use and reach a wider audience.

Continuous Learning and Improvement

- Ongoing Education: Promote ongoing learning and professional growth in the field of artificial intelligence by providing users with resources to keep up to current on new advancements.
- Knowledge Sharing: Encourage an environment in which people routinely share their experiences and insights related to artificial intelligence within enterprises.
- Evaluation and Feedback: Consistently assess the success of educational initiatives, and adapt their design in response to user input and technical developments.

5.9 Environmental Impact for Control Points of AI/ML

Sustainable development necessitates an understanding of and approach to regulating AI/ML (Artificial Intelligence/Machine Intelligence) technologies' environmental impact. The following

Applications of Artificial Intelligence and Machine Learning are important tactics for determining and minimizing the environmental impact at AI/ML control points:

Figure.5.4 Environmental Impact for Control Points of AI/ML

Energy Consumption

- Create and implement algorithms that are less computationally demanding and more energy-efficient.

- Hardware Optimization: Reduce power usage by using energy-efficient hardware and optimizing currently installed hardware.

- Invest in green data centers that employ energy-saving technologies and make use of renewable energy sources.

Carbon Footprint Reduction

- Carbon Offsetting: To make up for the carbon emissions produced by AI/ML activities, invest in carbon offsetting projects.
- Renewable Energy: Use renewable energy sources like solar, wind, and hydroelectric power to run data centers and AI/ML systems.
- Energy Management Systems: Use energy management systems to keep an eye on and lower AI/ML systems' carbon footprint.

Sustainable Development

- Sustainable Practices: Use sustainable techniques, such utilizing recycled materials and cutting down on technological waste, into the design and implementation of AI systems.
- Lifetime Assessment: To comprehend the environmental impact of AI systems from development to disposal, carry out lifetime evaluations.
- Circular Economy: Recycle and reuse hardware parts and resources to advance a circular economy.

Environmental Impact Assessments

- Impact Analysis: To investigate the possible environmental implications of AI/ML initiatives, conduct environmental impact assessments (EIAs).
- Regulation Compliance: To reduce the adverse effects on ecosystems, make sure that environmental regulations and standards are followed.

- Risk management: To address and reduce environmental concerns connected to AI/ML systems, create risk management plans.

Data Management

- Reduce the quantity of data that is processed and stored by implementing data minimization techniques. This will cut down on energy usage.

- Efficient Data Storage: Make use of energy- and space-efficient data storage options.

- Data Center Location: Take into account the physical location of data centers, such as those in colder areas, to reduce the need for cooling and electricity.

Collaboration and Partnerships

- Industry Cooperation: Work with colleagues in the field to create and implement best practices that will lessen artificial intelligence's negative environmental effects.

- Research Collaborations: Join forces with academic and scientific establishments to investigate novel approaches aimed at reducing the ecological impact of artificial intelligence technologies.

- Participate in government programs designed to advance sustainable practices and green technologies.

Environmental Awareness and Education

- Training Programs: Put in place training initiatives to inform staff members and other interested parties about the environmental effects of artificial intelligence and sustainable practices.

- Public Awareness: Promote responsible use and educate the public about the environmental effects of AI and MI.

- Corporate Responsibility: Promote an environmentally conscious culture inside companies, stressing the significance of sustainability in the advancement of artificial intelligence.

Monitoring and Reporting

- Environmental Metrics: Create and monitor environmental metrics, such as energy use, carbon emissions, and electronic waste, to assess the effects of AI systems.

- Sustainability Reporting: Consistently release reports outlining the effects of artificial intelligence activities on the environment and the steps taken to alleviate those effects.

- Continuous Improvement: Create a structure for ongoing environmental performance enhancement, utilizing monitoring data to guide choices.

Innovation and Technology

- Invest in the study and creation of green artificial intelligence (AI) technologies with an eye on reducing their negative environmental effects.

- Effective and Efficient AI Models: Create AI models that minimize the requirement for a lot of processing power.

Applications of Artificial Intelligence and Machine Learning

- Optimization Strategies: Apply optimization strategies to improve AI operations' efficiency and lower energy usage.

Policy and Regulation

- Environmental Policies: Create and implement regulations that require AI development and application to follow sustainable principles.

- Regulatory Compliance: Make sure AI systems abide by local, national, and international environmental norms and standards.

- Encourage the adoption of environmentally friendly AI techniques and technology by organizations by pushing for incentives and assistance.

5.10 Global Collaboration for Control Points of AI/ML

In order to ensure that AI/ML (Artificial Intelligence/Machine Intelligence) systems are developed and used responsibly, ethically, and sustainably, global collaboration is required for managing control points of these systems. The following are methods and techniques for encouraging international cooperation:

International Standards and Frameworks

- Create worldwide Standards: Work with international organizations to create and implement worldwide guidelines for the safety, ethics, and governance of artificial intelligence.

- Harmonize Regulations: To maintain uniformity and prevent regulatory arbitrage, endeavor to harmonize AI regulations throughout nations.

- Support and take part in the development of AI-related standards by associations such as IEEE (Institute of Electrical and Electronics Engineers) and ISO (International Organization for Standardization).

Multilateral Organizations and Agreements

- UN Initiatives: Take part in UN programs like the Sustainable Development Goals (SDGs) and UNESCO's ethical guidelines for AI.

- Observe the AI principles set forth by the Organization for Economic Co-operation and Development (OECD), which encourage the responsible development and application of AI.

- G20 and G7 Summits: Encourage international cooperation by promoting AI-related talks and agreements at these summits.

Cross-Border Research and Development

- International Research Consortiums: Establish international research consortiums to share resources and knowledge while working together on AI research and development.

- Collaborative Research Initiatives: Launch collaborative research initiatives including academic institutions, business, and governments from many nations.

Applications of Artificial Intelligence and Machine Learning

- Global Innovation centers: Create international centers for collaboration on cutting-edge AI technologies amongst academics and developers from different countries.

Data Sharing and Privacy

- Cross-Border Data Flows: Provide frameworks to enable safe, privacy-abiding cross-border data transfers, promoting global cooperation while safeguarding personal information.

- Agreements on Data Governance: To guarantee moral and responsible data sharing, negotiate international accords on data governance.

- Privacy Standards: To guarantee data protection in cross-border partnerships, conform to international privacy standards like the General Data Protection Regulation (GDPR).

Capacity Building and Knowledge Sharing

- International Training Programs: Put in place international training programs to strengthen emerging nations' AI capabilities and guarantee fair access to AI resources and expertise.

- Knowledge sharing Platforms: Establish knowledge sharing platforms so that nations can exchange research findings, best practices, and AI technical innovations.

- International Conferences: Arrange and take part in global gatherings that center on technology, ethics, and governance in artificial intelligence.

Ethical and Responsible AI

- Global Ethical Guidelines: Create and advance global ethical standards for artificial intelligence to make sure that these systems are in line with society norms and human values.

- International ethics committees should be established to supervise the development and application of AI and to offer advice on moral matters.

- Cultural Sensitivity: Make sure AI systems are inclusive and sensitive to other cultural viewpoints and values.

AI for Social Good

- Global Challenges: Work together to use AI to solve global issues including healthcare, poverty reduction, and climate change.

- AI for SDGs: Use AI to further the Sustainable Development Goals of the United Nations, fostering sustainability and well-being around the world.

- Humanitarian AI Initiatives: Encourage and participate in AI initiatives that benefit marginalized and vulnerable communities around the globe.

Regulatory Cooperation

- Policy Dialogue: Encourage policy discussions among nations to address shared opportunities and difficulties around AI laws.

- International regulatory sandboxes should be established so that nations can test and assess AI laws in a safe setting.

Applications of Artificial Intelligence and Machine Learning

- Compliance Frameworks: Create globally known and agreed compliance frameworks to make it easier for multinational AI projects to comply with regulations.

Public-Private Partnerships

- Create international industry coalitions to work together, pooling resources and knowledge, to address AI-related issues.

- Establish cooperative platforms so that businesses, governments, and civil society can collaborate on AI innovation and governance.

- Finance and Investment: Promote global financing and investment in artificial intelligence initiatives that give ethical and sustainable development first priority.

Monitoring and Evaluation

- Create worldwide mechanisms to keep an eye on the effectiveness and effects of AI systems and make sure they adhere to safety and ethical guidelines.

- Impact Assessments: To determine how AI technology will affect society, the economy, and the environment, conduct global impact assessments.

Feedback Mechanisms: Provide worldwide channels for stakeholders to voice issues and offer suggestions about AI policies and systems.

6. General Working of AI /ML

The terms artificial intelligence (AI) and machine learning (ML) refer to a wide range of methods and tools that make it possible for machines to carry out tasks that ordinarily call for human intelligence. An outline of how AI/ML systems function is provided here:

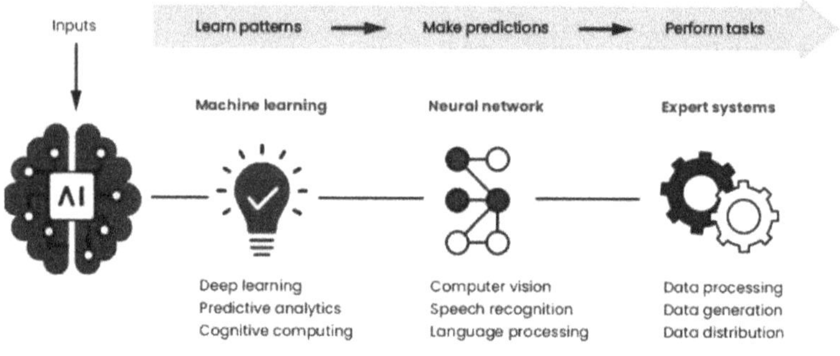

Figure.6.1 General working of AI /ML

6.1 Data Collection and Preparation for General working of AI /ML

Since the quality of the data directly affects the performance and dependability of the models, data preparation and collection are essential stages in the development of AI/ML systems. The following is a comprehensive how-to guide for gathering and preparing data for AI/ML projects:

Data Collection

Sources of Data

Applications of Artificial Intelligence and Machine Learning

- Databases: Gather information from data warehouses, relational databases, and NoSQL databases.

- Web APIs: To retrieve data from internet services (such as social media sites, financial services, and meteorological data), use web APIs.

- Web scraping: Use web scraping libraries and tools (like Beautiful Soup and Scrapy) to extract data from webpages.

- Collect information from Internet of Things (IoT) networks, smart devices, and physical sensors.

- User-Generated Content: Gather information created by users, such as discussion threads, reviews, and interaction records.

- Use publicly available datasets from academic institutions, governments, and other organizations (e.g., Kaggle, UCI Machine Learning Repository).

Types of Data

- Structured Data: Usually seen in spreadsheets and SQL databases, structured data is arranged in rows and columns.

- Unstructured data refers to unformatted data, including text, image, audio, and video files.

- Semi-Structured Data: JSON and XML files are examples of data that has certain organizational characteristics.

Data Preparation

Data Cleaning

- Managing Missing Values: Make use of methods like deletion (getting rid of rows or columns containing missing values) or imputation (filling in missing values with mean, median, or mode).

- Eliminating Duplicates: To preserve data integrity, find and eliminate duplicate records.

- Error Correction: Recognize and fix data inconsistencies, errors, and outliers.

Data Transformation

- Scale numerical features to a conventional range, such as [0, 1] or [-1, 1], using the normalization technique.

- Standardization: Assign a mean of 0 and a standard deviation of 1 to the features.

- Coding Qualitative Variables:

- One-Hot Encoding: Generate binary vectors from category variables.

- Label Encoding: Give every category a distinct number.

- Feature engineering involves generating new features (such as extracting date components from timestamps or developing interaction terms) from current data in order to better capture underlying trends.

Data Integration

- Combining several datasets into a single dataset by using shared keys or characteristics is known as dataset merging.

Applications of Artificial Intelligence and Machine Learning

- Data Aggregation: To generate new metrics or features (e.g., calculating average monthly sales), summarize or integrate data.

Data Reduction

- Feature Selection: To lower dimensionality and boost model performance, find and pick the most pertinent features.

- Dimensionality Reduction: To cut down on features without sacrificing crucial information, apply methods like Principal Component Analysis (PCA).

Exploratory Data Analysis (EDA)

- To comprehend the distribution and relationships of data, compute descriptive statistics metrics like mean, median, standard deviation, and correlation.

- Data visualization: Examine data distributions visually to spot trends or abnormalities using plots like heat maps, box plots, scatter plots, and histograms.

Data Splitting

- The section of the dataset used to train the model is known as the training set.

- A distinct section of the dataset called the validation set is utilized to adjust the model's hyper parameters and avoid overfitting.

- Test Set: A separate subset of the dataset that is used to assess the performance of the finished model.

6.2 Feature Engineering for General working of AI /ML

Using domain expertise, feature engineering is the process of extracting or creating additional features from unprocessed data in order to enhance machine learning model performance. This stage of the AI/ML pipeline is crucial because well-designed features can result in models that are more precise and useful. This is a thorough synopsis of feature engineering:

Figure.6.2 Feature Engineering for General working of AI /ML

Understanding the Data and the Problem

Understanding the dataset and the particular issue you are attempting to solve in detail is essential before you begin feature engineering. This includes:

- Domain Knowledge: Being aware of the details and context of the data.
- Finding patterns, trends, and connections in the data is known as exploratory data analysis, or EDA.

Types of Features

Numerical Features

- Using the data's preexisting numerical values directly is known as "original numerical features."
- Aggregated Features: Count, max, min, mean, and sum of data points over a specified group are summarized.
- Features that have been normalized or standardized involve scaling them to a typical distribution or range.

Categorical Features

- Authentic Categorical Features: Preserving the original categorical data.
- Features Encoded:
    - One-Hot Encoding: Creating binary vectors from categories.
    - Label encoding is the process of giving categories numerical numbers.
    - Converting categories into binary numbers is known as binary encoding.

Text Features

- Word frequencies are used to represent text data in a bag of words, or Bow.
- Word frequencies are scaled by the inverse document frequency using the term frequency-inverse document frequency (TF-IDF) method.
- Word embedding: Words are represented in a dense vector space using pre-trained word vectors (e.g., Word2Vec, Glove).

- N-grams are features made up of groups of N words or letters.

Time Features

- The process of obtaining date/time components from timestamps, including the year, month, day, hour, minute, and second.
- Cycle-based features: utilizing sine and cosine transformations to represent time-based information in a cycle (e.g., day of the week, month of the year).

Creating New Features

Mathematical Transformations

- Creating polynomial combinations of numerical characteristics and interaction terms are known as polynomial features.
- Logarithmic and Exponential Transformations: To address skewness, logarithmic or exponential functions are applied to numerical features.

Aggregations and Groupings

- Group aggregations: computing statistics (count, mean, and sum) for data groups (e.g., mean amount purchased per customer).
- Developing features based on aggregated time periods or rolling windows (e.g., average sales over the last seven days).

Interaction Features

Applications of Artificial Intelligence and Machine Learning

- Combining features to record their interactions (such as the product of two features) is known as feature combination.
- Cross Features: Producing cross-product features to record categorical variable interactions.

Dimensionality Reduction

Techniques

- Keeping variance intact while reducing dimensionality is possible with principal component analysis (PCA).
- Reducing dimensionality while maintaining class reparability is what linear discriminant analysis, or LDA, does.
- T-SNE: A technique for reducing dimensionality in stochastic neighbor embedding.

Handling Missing Values

Imputation Strategies

- Mode, Median, and Mean Imputation: Using the feature's mean, median, or mode to fill up any missing values.
- Filling gaps by propagating the next or previous value is known as forward/backward filling.
- Using a machine learning model to forecast and fill in missing values is known as predictive imputation.

Feature Selection

Techniques

- Filter Methods: Choosing features by statistical tests (e.g., Chi-Square, ANOVA).

- Wrapper Methods: Recursive Feature Elimination, for example, use model performance to pick features.

- Embedded Methods: Making use of methods (like Lasso and Ridge) that choose features during model training.

6.3 Model Selection for General working of AI /ML

Model selection is a crucial step in the machine learning pipeline. It involves choosing the most appropriate algorithm for your specific problem based on the nature of the data, the problem type, and the desired outcomes. Here's a comprehensive guide on how to approach model selection:

Understand the Problem Type

Figure.6.3 Understand the Problem Type

Supervised Learning

- Classification: Forecasting labels (e.g., emails marked as spam or not).

Applications of Artificial Intelligence and Machine Learning

- Predicting continuous values (like home prices) is known as regression.

Unsupervised Learning

- Clustering: Combining comparable data pieces (e.g., segmenting customers).
- Reducing the dimensionality of a feature set (e.g., PCA).
- Finding anomalies or peculiar patterns (e.g., fraud detection) is known as anomaly detection.

Semi-Supervised Learning

- Using both labeled and unlabeled data (e.g., text classification with limited labeled data) is known as partially labeled data.

Reinforcement Learning

- Making decisions: figuring out how to play games or use robots to maximize cumulative benefits.

Consider the Nature of the Data

Data Size

- Small Datasets: Decision trees or linear regression are examples of simple models.
- Huge Datasets: Ensemble techniques, deep learning models, etc.

Feature Types

- Algorithms that perform well with continuous data, such as support vector machines and linear regression, are examples of numerical features.
- Algorithms that can handle categorical data, such as decision trees and random forests, are referred to as categorical features.

Data Distribution

- Linearity: For linear relationships, use linear models.
- Non-Linearity: For intricate interactions, employ non-linear models (such as neural networks and SVM with non-linear kernels).

Common Algorithms and Their Use Cases

Classification

- Problems with binary categorization using logistic regression.
- K-Nearest Neighbors (KNN): Ideal for small datasets, KNN is easy to understand and apply.
- SVMs, or support vector machines, work well in high-dimensional spaces.
- Decision trees are easy-to-understand models.
- Random Forests: An ensemble technique that lowers overfitting and increases accuracy.
- Gradient Boosting: Excellent performance with structured data (e.g., Boost, LightGBM).
- Neural Networks: useful for intricate patterns, particularly when working with big datasets.

Applications of Artificial Intelligence and Machine Learning

Regression

- Linear Regression: Straightforward linear correlations.
- Ridge/Lasso Regression: Regularized linear regression.
- Non-linear correlations in decision trees.
- Random Forests: Group technique for tasks involving regression.
- Gradient Boosting: Excellent results while performing regression tasks.
- Neural networks are useful for intricate patterns.

Clustering

- K-Means: Easy to use and effective with big datasets.
- Ideal for tiny datasets and hierarchical relationships is hierarchical clustering.
- DBSCAN: Good at handling noise and clusters of any shape.

Dimensionality Reduction

- PCA stands for principal component analysis, which reduces dimensionality linearly.
- Stochastic Neighbor Embedding with t-Distribution (t-SNE): Reducing nonlinear dimensionality is beneficial for visual aids.
- Auto encoders: Diminished dimensionality via neural networks.

Model Evaluation and Selection

Cross-Validation

- K-Fold Cross-Validation involves training the model k times after partitioning the data into k subgroups.
- Cross-Validation with One out (LOOCV): a unique instance of k-fold cross-validation where k is the quantity of data points.

Performance Metrics

- Classification: ROC-AUC, F1 score, recall, accuracy, and precision.
- R-squared, Mean Squared Error (MSE), and Mean Absolute Error (MAE) are used in regression.
- Clustering: Davies-Bold in index, Silhouette score.
- Reduction of Dimensionality: Reconstruction error and explained variance.

Model Complexity and Interpretability

Simple Models

- Advantages: Faster training and easier to understand.
- Cons: Complex data may be under fit.

Complex Models

- Advantages: Better precision and ability to capture intricate patterns.
- Cons: More difficult to understand, requires longer training sessions, and may over fit.

6.4 Model Training for General working of AI /ML

Applications of Artificial Intelligence and Machine Learning The process of teaching a machine learning algorithm to make judgments or predictions based on data is known as model training. Using a training dataset, the model's parameters are optimized, and the model's performance is assessed to make sure it generalizes well to new, untested data. This is a thorough guide to model training:

Figure.6.4 Model Training for General working of AI /ML

Prepare the Data

Data Splitting

- Training Set: The subset of the data that the model is trained on.

- Validation Set: The section where hyper parameters are adjusted and overfitting is avoided.

- Test Set: The section utilized to assess the ultimate performance of the model.

Choose a Model

Based on the nature of the problem (classification, regression, clustering, etc.), the properties of the data, and the project specifications, choose the best machine learning algorithm.

Define the Model

To specify the model architecture, use tools and frameworks (such as scikit-learn, Tensor Flow, and PyTorch). This entails defining the kind of model and its specifications.

Initialize Model Parameters

For many algorithms, initial parameters are set automatically, but for some complex models (e.g., neural networks), you may need to specify initial weights and biases.

Specify the Loss Function

- To specify the model architecture, use tools and frameworks (such as scikit-learn, Tensor Flow, and PyTorch).
- This entails defining the kind of model and its specifications.

Choose an Optimization Algorithm

The model's parameters are changed by optimization methods in order to minimize the loss function. Typical algorithms for optimization consist of:

- Gradient Descent: This method of iteratively updating parameters involves traveling in the direction of the loss function's negative gradient.

- Stochastic Gradient Descent (SGD): This technique expedites computation by updating parameters using a random subset of the data.
- Adam: combines momentum with the advantages of both RMSProp and SGD, frequently resulting in faster convergence.

Train the Model

Forward Propagation

- Input Data: To produce predictions, run the model on the training set of data.
- Compute Loss: Make use of the loss function to determine the loss.

Backward Propagation

- Compute Gradients: Determine the loss function's gradients in relation to the model's parameters.
- Update Parameters: Using the gradients and the selected optimization procedure, modify the model's parameters.

Iterations (Epochs and Batches)

- Epoch: A single run of the whole training set.
- Batch: A portion of the training data used in a single parameter update iteration.

Monitor Training

To keep an eye on the model's performance during training, track measures like accuracy and loss. For visualization, use programs such as Tensor Board.

Hyper parameter Tuning

Use methods like these to optimize hyper parameters (such learning rate, batch size, and number of layers):

- Grid Search: Methodically examining various hyper parameter combinations.
- Selecting combinations of hyper parameters at random for testing is known as random search.
- Bayesian Optimization: Determining the ideal hyper parameters through the use of probabilistic models.

Regularization

Avoid overfitting by using regularization strategies:

- L1/L2 Regularization: Increases the loss function's penalty in proportion to the model parameters' squared or absolute values.
- In order to keep neural networks from overfitting, dropout involves randomly removing neurons during training.
- Early Stopping: When the model's performance begins to deteriorate on the validation set, training is stopped.

Evaluate the Model

Using the proper assessment measures, determine how well the model performed on the test set:

Applications of Artificial Intelligence and Machine Learning

- Classification: ROC-AUC, F1 score, recall, accuracy, and precision.
- R-squared, Mean Squared Error (MSE), and Mean Absolute Error (MAE) are used in regression.

Model Deployment

Move the model to a production environment so it can make predictions on fresh data after it has been trained and assessed.

6.5 Deployment for General working of AI /ML

The process of enabling a trained machine learning model to be used in a production setting, where it may make predictions on fresh data, is known as deployment. Choosing the deployment environment, guaranteeing scalability, keeping an eye on performance, and maintaining the model are all necessary for a successful deployment. Here is a thorough overview of the deployment procedure:

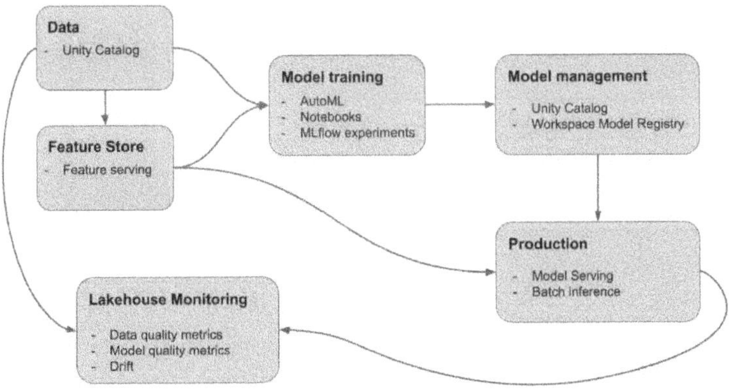

Figure.6.5 Deployment for General working of AI /ML

Preparation

Model Export

- Conserve the learned model in a deployment-ready format (.h5,.pkl, ONNX, etc.).

```
# For TensorFlow/Keras models
model.save('model.h5')


# For scikit-learn models
import joblib
joblib.dump(model, 'model.pkl')
```

Choose a Deployment Environment

On-Premises

- Install the model on nearby servers.
- Ideal for settings where data privacy regulations are stringent.

Cloud

- Install the model on AWS, Azure, and Google Cloud platforms.
- Provides managed services, flexibility, and scalability for model serving.

Edge Devices

- Install the model on peripherals such as IoT and smartphone devices.
- Appropriate for low-latency, real-time prediction.

Deployment Methods

Batch Processing

- Process a lot of data at predetermined intervals.
- Ideal for non-instantaneous applications such as monthly summaries.

Real-Time Processing

- As soon as data is obtained, make forecasts.
- Ideal for applications like fraud detection that need quick answers.

Model Serving

REST API

- Utilize a RESTful API to serve the model.
- Enables other apps to communicate with the model via HTTP.

GRPC

- For high-performance, low-latency communication, serve the model using gRPC.

Model Serving Frameworks

- To serve the model, use frameworks such as Torch Serve, Tensor Flow Serving, or FastAPI.

```
# Example using FastAPI for a scikit-learn model
from fastapi import FastAPI
```

```python
import joblib
app = FastAPI()
model = joblib.load('model.pkl')
@app.post('/predict')
def predict(data: List[float]):
    prediction = model.predict([data])
    return {'prediction': prediction[0]}
```

Scalability and Reliability

Load Balancing

- Divide up incoming requests among several model instances.
- Make sure it is very dependable and available.

Auto-Scaling

- Adapt the number of model instances automatically to the load.
- Adapt to changing traffic conditions well.

Monitoring and Logging

Performance Monitoring

- Monitor important parameters such as error rates, throughput, and latency.
- Make use of tools such as Grafana, Prometheus, or monitoring services dedicated to cloud providers.

Logging

Applications of Artificial Intelligence and Machine Learning

- For auditing and debugging purposes, keep track of prediction requests and answers.
- Make use of cloud provider-specific logging services or logging frameworks such as Logstash and Fluentd.

Model Management

Versioning

- Continue to use several model iterations.
- Enables rolling back to earlier iterations when necessary

```
# Example versioning in TensorFlow
model.save('model_v1.h5')
model.save('model_v2.h5')
```

A/B Testing

- Install different iterations of the model at the same time.
- To choose the finest one, compare their performances.

Continuous Integration/Continuous Deployment (CI/CD)

- Use CI/CD pipelines to automate the deployment process.
- It is possible to leverage tools like Jenkins, GitHub Actions, and Git Lab CI/CD.

Security

Authentication and Authorization

- Use appropriate authorization and authentication procedures to safeguard the model API.

- Make use of OAuth, tokens, API keys, etc.

Data Encryption

To guarantee security and privacy, encrypt data both in transit and at rest.

6.6 Monitoring and Maintenance for General working of AI /ML

Upkeep and monitoring are essential stages in the lifecycle of an AI/ML system. They guarantee that the model will always be dependable, accurate, and effective. Here is a thorough explanation of the procedures involved:

Monitoring

Performance Monitoring

- Accuracy: Make constant assessments of the model's accuracy using fresh data.
- Latency: Check that the time it takes to make forecasts satisfies performance requirements by measuring it.
- Throughput: Keep track of how many forecasts are made in a certain amount of time.
- Error Rates: Keep track of the quantity and kind of errors that occur (such as incorrect data processing or failed predictions).

Data Drift Detection

- Concept drift is the result of a target variable's statistical characteristics changing over time.

Applications of Artificial Intelligence and Machine Learning

- Covariate Drift: Occurs when the input features' statistical characteristics alter over time.
- Detection Methods: Employ strategies including utilizing statistical tests like the Kolmogorov-Smirnov test, establishing control charts, and keeping an eye on feature distributions.

Model Drift Detection

- Track variations in the model's predictions over time with Prediction Drift.
- Performance Decline: Monitor important performance indicators to determine whether the model's performance is declining.

Logging

- Keep track of your input data, forecasts, and actual results in prediction logs.
- Error Logs: Record any exceptions or mistakes that happen while making a prediction.

Alerting

Create automated alerts to inform relevant parties when there are major changes to the model's performance or the properties of the data.

Maintenance

Retraining

- Regularly retrain the model using fresh data (e.g., daily, weekly, monthly) is known as scheduled retraining.
- Triggered Retraining: Retrain the model in response to severe data drift detection or when performance metrics drop below a predetermined threshold.

Model Versioning

- Version Control: Monitor various iterations of the model.
- Rollback: The option to go back to an earlier version of the model in case the performance of the current version is subpar.

Hyper parameter Tuning

- Continuous Tuning: To maintain peak performance, periodically review and adjust hyper parameters.
- Automated Tuning: To determine the ideal hyper parameters, use technologies for automated hyper parameter tuning.

Updating Features

- Feature Engineering: To make sure feature engineering procedures are still applicable, they should be regularly reviewed and updated.
- Feature Selection: Evaluate features on a regular basis, adding or removing features as needed.

Model Interpretability

- Explainability: Make sure the model can be understood in the long run. To explain model predictions, use methods

Applications of Artificial Intelligence and Machine Learning such as SHAP (SHapley Additive exPlanations) or LIME (Local Interpretable Model-agnostic Explanations).

- Transparency: Keep records and logs that shed light on the choices and modifications made to the model.

Security

- Data Privacy: Make sure that laws pertaining to data privacy are consistently followed.
- Model Security: Prevent unwanted access and hostile attacks on the model.

Tools and Frameworks

Monitoring Tools

- Prometheus: A well-liked toolbox for alerting and monitoring.
- Grafana: A program used frequently with Prometheus for data visualization.
- ELK Stack: Kibana, Logstash, and Elasticsearch for monitoring and logging.

Data Drift Detection Tools

- Alibi identify is a Python package designed to identify drift in concepts and data.
- Evidently: A production monitoring and analysis tool for machine learning models.

Model Management Platforms

- An open-source platform called ML flow is used to oversee the whole machine learning lifecycle.
- Kube flow: A set of machine learning tools for Kubernetes that makes managing and deploying models easier.

CI/CD for ML

- Jenkins: A CI/CD pipeline building open-source automation server.
- Git Lab CI/CD: Configured to work with Git Lab repositories.
- Circle CI: A CI/CD tool hosted in the cloud.

AI/ML models continue to produce dependable and accurate predictions in production by putting strong monitoring and maintenance procedures in place. This entails managing data and model drift, retraining on a regular basis, tracking performance continuously, and upholding security and transparency. These procedures can be greatly streamlined with the right tools and frameworks, guaranteeing the long-term viability of your AI/ML systems.

7. Edge Computing of Future ML

The deployment of machine learning (ML) applications is becoming more and more dependent on edge computing, particularly as the need for real-time processing and low latency responses increases. With this paradigm, data processing is moved from centralized cloud servers to edge devices that are localized, like local servers, cellphones, and Internet of Things gadgets. An outline of how edge computing will influence machine learning in the future is provided below:

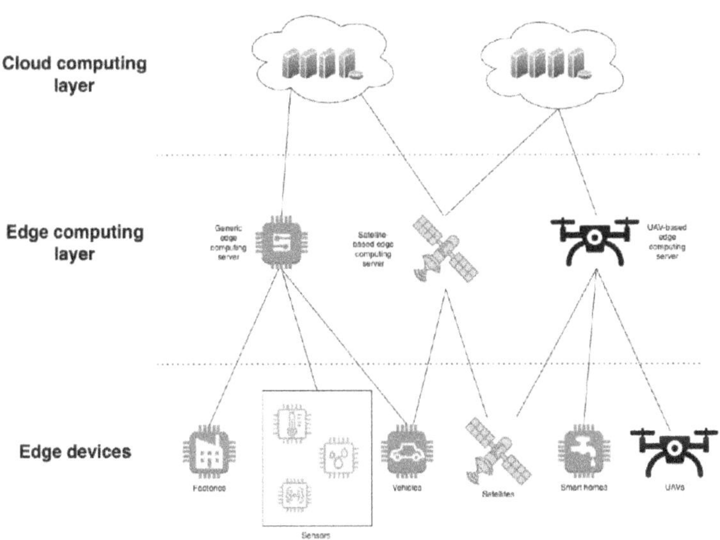

Figure.7.1 Edge computing of future ML

7.1 Benefits of Edge Computing for ML for Edge computing of future ML

As machine learning (ML) develops, edge computing has a number of noteworthy advantages. The main benefits are as follows:

- Decreased Latency: Edge computing drastically cuts latency by processing data near to the source, making real-time responses possible for applications like industrial automation, driverless cars, and real-time analytics.

- Enhanced Security and Privacy: Local data processing on edge devices lowers the possibility of data breaches and improves security. In delicate industries like healthcare and banking, where data privacy is crucial, this is especially crucial.

- Bandwidth Efficiency: By minimizing the need to send massive amounts of data to centralized data centers, edge computing lowers the amount of bandwidth used and the expenses related to it. Applications with expensive or restricted connectivity alternatives will benefit from this.

- Reliability and resilience: Edge devices have the ability to function without the assistance of central servers, therefore they will continue to function even in the event of a network connection loss. For mission-critical applications like industrial controls and emergency response systems, this reliability is essential.

- Scalability: Scalable machine learning solutions may handle growing volumes of data and computation without taxing central resources by dividing computational duties among several edge devices.

- Energy Efficiency: By eliminating the need for data centers and potentially energy-intensive long-distance data transmission, local data processing can be more energy-efficient.

- Context Awareness and Personalization: By adapting machine learning models to particular situations and settings, Edge devices can provide users more relevant and tailored services based on their data and immediate surroundings.

- Cost Reduction: Businesses and organizations can reduce operational expenses associated with ML solution deployment by lowering data transfer quantities and reducing dependency on centralized cloud infrastructure. This makes ML solutions more affordable.

As machine learning (ML) advances, combining it with edge computing will improve applications' scalability, security, and efficiency. This will spur innovation in domains including smart cities, the Internet of Things (IoT), autonomous systems, and personalized healthcare.

7.2 Challenges in Edge Computing for Edge computing of future ML

Figure.7.1 Challenges in Edge Computing for Edge computing of future ML

Although edge computing has several advantages for machine learning (ML), there are also a number of issues that need to be resolved, particularly as the technology advances. The following are the main obstacles:

- Resource Restraints: In comparison to centralized cloud data centers, edge devices usually have less memory, storage, and processing power. Large datasets and complex machine learning models may perform more slowly as a result of this limitation.

- Scalability: It might be difficult and complex to coordinate and manage a big number of dispersed edge devices. Complex administration systems are needed to update ML models and guarantee consistent performance across numerous devices.

- Diversity and Quality of Data: Edge devices may gather noisy, heterogeneous data from a variety of sources. Although difficult, ensuring data consistency and quality for inference and training is essential.

- Model Deployment and Updates: Compared to centralized systems, it is more difficult to deploy and maintain ML models on edge devices. Effective rollback, versioning, and model distribution procedures are needed for this.

- Security and Privacy: Although processing data locally using edge computing can improve data privacy, protecting a large number of dispersed edge devices from cyberattacks is difficult. It is crucial to guarantee end-to-end security, which includes secure communication routes and device authentication.

- Energy Consumption: Even though edge computing has the potential to be more energy-efficient, edge devices still need to weigh the computational demands against the power requirements, particularly in locations that rely on batteries or have limited electricity.

- Interoperability: There may be problems with interoperability because different manufacturers' edge devices may use different protocols and standards. An ecosystem for edge computing cannot function well unless there is smooth communication and interaction across disparate devices.

- Real-Time Processing: It can be difficult to guarantee real-time data processing and decision-making on edge devices with constrained resources. It is essential to optimize hardware and algorithms for low latency performance.

- Data Synchronization: When there is sporadic or unstable connectivity, synchronizing data between edge devices and the central cloud can be challenging.

- Maintenance and Support: Compared to controlling centralized infrastructure, maintaining and supporting a dispersed network of edge devices can be more difficult and expensive.

Innovative approaches to network administration, security protocols, hardware design, and software development are needed to meet these problems. Overcoming these challenges will be crucial to utilizing edge computing and machine learning to the fullest extent possible as these technologies develop.

7.3 Technologies Enabling Edge Computing for Edge computing of future ML

Figure.7.2 Technologies Enabling Edge Computing for Edge computing of future ML

Edge computing is made possible by a number of technologies, especially in light of machine learning's (ML) future. Following are a few of the major technologies:

- Edge AI Chips: Specialized hardware, including Google's Edge TPU, Intel's Movidius, and NVIDIA's Jetson series, is made to efficiently handle AI and ML tasks on edge devices. These chips are appropriate for edge computing because they offer great performance at minimal power consumption.

- 5G Networks: High bandwidth, low latency, and dependable connectivity are provided by the 5G network deployment, and these features are critical for real-time data processing and communication between edge devices and central servers.

- Internet of Things (IoT) Devices: IoT devices gather and process data at the edge using sensors and actuators. Because they allow for data gathering and initial processing closer to the source, these devices are essential to edge computing.

- Fog Computing: A further development of cloud computing, fog computing uses a decentralized computing infrastructure with data, computation, storage, and apps dispersed between the cloud and the data source in the most sensible and effective locations. This enhances processing efficiency and lowers latency.

- Micro services and containerization: Docker and Kubernetes are two technologies that make it possible to deploy and operate isolated, lightweight environments (containers) on edge devices. Development of ML applications is made modular and scalable by the micro services design.

- Machine Learning Frameworks for Edge: ML models may be executed on edge devices with the help of frameworks like Edge Impulse, OpenVINO, and TensorFlow Lite. The creation, implementation, and optimization of ML models for edge contexts are made easier by these frameworks.

- Platforms for Distributed Computing: By enabling distributed data processing and ML model training across numerous edge and cloud nodes, platforms such as TensorFlow Distributed, Apache Spark, and Kafka improve scalability and performance.

- Edge Analytics: Without depending on centralized cloud resources, real-time insights and decision-making capabilities can be obtained using advanced analytics tools and platforms that can process data at the edge.

- Edge Orchestration: Platforms for orchestration oversee and manage the lifespan, scaling, and deployment of applications across edge devices. AWS IoT Greengrass, Google Cloud IoT Edge, and Microsoft Azure IoT Edge are a few examples.

- Security Solutions: Data and models on edge devices are protected against cyber-attacks by strong security technologies such as encryption, secure boot, and hardware-based security modules (e.g., TPM).

- Advanced embedded systems enable effective data processing and machine learning inference at the edge by combining sensors, processors, and communication modules into a single device.

By working together, these technologies enable the creation and application of edge computing solutions, allowing for the benefits of edge computing to be utilized for machine learning and other applications.

7.4 Use Cases of Edge Computing in ML for Edge computing of future ML

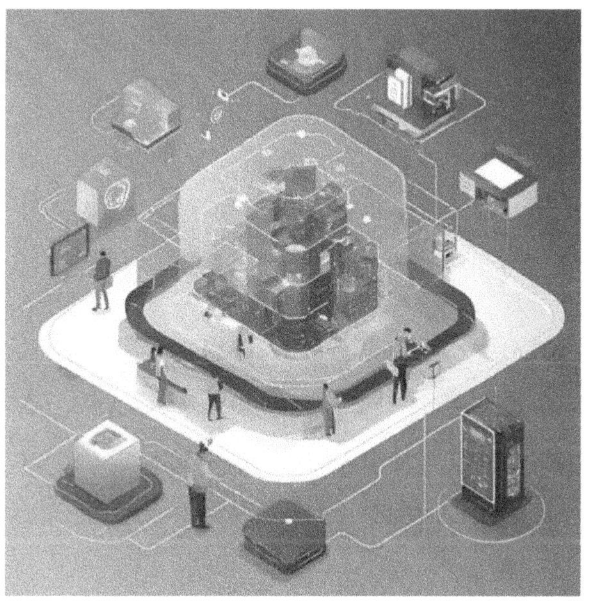

Figure.7.3 Use Cases of Edge Computing in ML for Edge computing of future ML

Machine learning (ML) offers many uses for edge computing, especially as the technology develops to meet the needs of new applications. Here are some important scenarios:

Autonomous Vehicles: Real-time processing of sensor data (from cameras and LIDAR, for example) is made possible via edge computing. The onboard computers in the car use ML models to make snap judgments regarding safety, obstacle avoidance, and navigation.

- Industrial Internet of Things (IIoT): In the manufacturing sector, edge computing uses data from factory floor sensors and machines to perform real-time monitoring, quality assurance, and predictive maintenance. To reduce downtime, machine learning models anticipate equipment breakdowns and identify irregularities.

- Healthcare: Real-time processing of patient data via wearables and edge-enabled medical equipment allows for the monitoring of vital signs, the identification of abnormalities, and the prompt alerting of healthcare personnel. As a result, crucial health actions happen with less delay.

- Smart Cities: Applications such as environmental monitoring, traffic control, and surveillance are made possible by edge computing. In order to improve public safety, monitor air quality, and optimize traffic flow, machine learning models analyze data from sensors and cameras.

- Retail: Edge devices are used in retail environments to optimize store layouts, manage inventory, and evaluate

Applications of Artificial Intelligence and Machine Learning

customer behavior. ML models operate on edge devices to enhance supply chain efficiency, identify theft, and offer customized recommendations.

- Agriculture: To monitor crop health, improve irrigation, and manage resources, edge computing analyzes data from sensors and drones in agricultural settings. With the use of ML models, precision farming may increase productivity while decreasing waste.

- Smart Homes: Edge computing is used by home automation systems to process data from smart devices such as appliances, security cameras, and thermostats. Personalized automation, energy management, and improved security are made possible by ML models.

- Remote Monitoring and Maintenance: Edge computing analyzes data locally to track the condition of equipment and anticipate malfunctions in remote places like wind farms and oil rigs. This enables preventive maintenance and lessens the requirement for continuous connectivity.

- AR and VR (augmented and virtual reality): Edge computing lowers latency by processing data locally to facilitate AR and VR applications. This improves the user experience for training simulations, gaming, and remote help.

- Telecommunications: To improve consumer experiences, optimize networks, and process data in real time, telecom businesses employ edge computing. Network traffic management, outage prediction, and service personalization are all made possible by ML models.

- Energy Management: To optimize energy distribution, identify problems, and control demand in real-time, edge computing is used in smart grids and energy management systems to interpret data from meters and sensors.

- Public safety and emergency response: In an emergency, edge devices can provide real-time insights by analyzing data from social media, cameras, and sensors. ML models help with resource allocation, threat detection, and crowd control.

These use cases demonstrate how edge computing may improve ML systems' scalability, performance, and efficiency across a range of industries, spurring innovation and enhancing results in practical situations.

7.5 Future Trends in Edge Computing for ML for Edge computing of future ML

The future of edge computing for machine learning (ML) is being shaped by a number of developments that are a reflection of changing application needs and technological advancements. Here are a few significant upcoming trends:

- Increasing Adoption of AI Chips: More specialized chips with lower power consumption for executing complicated machine learning models locally will be available. These processors are made for edge devices.

- Improved 5G Connectivity: As 5G networks continue to be deployed, they will offer the bandwidth and low latency required to handle increasingly complex edge

Applications of Artificial Intelligence and Machine Learning

computing applications. This will allow real-time data processing and a smooth interaction with cloud services.

- Federated Learning: Without requiring the sharing of raw data, federated learning enables ML models to be trained across numerous decentralized devices or servers. This method improves security and privacy of data, which makes it perfect for edge computing settings.

- Edge-to-Cloud Integration: By enabling hybrid architectures where data and machine learning models may be dynamically managed and processed across the edge and cloud, seamless integration between edge and cloud computing will maximize performance and resource usage.

- Edge AI Frameworks and Toolkits: ML model deployment and administration on edge devices will be made easier with the creation of more advanced and user-friendly edge AI frameworks and toolkits. Edge Impulse, Open VINO, and Tensor Flow Lite are a few examples.

- Edge-Orchestrated Services: To ensure effective resource usage and reliable performance, advanced orchestration platforms will oversee and automate the deployment, scaling, and upgrading of machine learning applications across dispersed edge environments.

- Security and Privacy Enhancements: To safeguard data and ML models from cyber-attacks and guarantee regulatory compliance, edge computing solutions will incorporate enhanced security protocols and privacy-preserving technology.

- Low-Power Edge Devices: The range and usefulness of edge computing will be expanded by the development of ultra-low-power edge devices, which will make it possible to deploy machine learning applications in energy-constrained situations like remote sensors and Internet of Things devices.

- Real-Time Analytics: As real-time analytics advances, edge devices will be able to process and analyze data instantly, giving rise to rapid insights and facilitating quicker decision-making in vital applications.

- Collaborative Edge Networks: To improve the precision and effectiveness of machine learning models, edge devices will cooperate more and more in collaborative networks, exchanging information and computing power. This is especially pertinent to applications such as self-driving cars and smart cities.

- Context-Aware Computing: Edge devices will become more contextually aware, using local data to offer tailored services that adjust to the unique requirements and circumstances of people or settings.

- Decentralized and Distributed AI: By enabling ML models to be trained and implemented across a variety of edge devices, decentralized and distributed AI will lessen dependency on centralized cloud infrastructure and improve scalability.

- Green computing initiatives will prioritize energy-efficient and sustainable computing methods, with an emphasis on minimizing edge computing's environmental impact

Applications of Artificial Intelligence and Machine Learning through resource optimization and the use of renewable energy sources.

These trends point to a future in which edge computing—by offering fast, effective, and secure data processing capabilities at the edge—will be essential in allowing sophisticated machine learning applications, spurring innovation, and revolutionizing entire industries.

7.6 Conclusion

By moving computation closer to the data source, edge computing is redefining the application of machine learning models. This change minimizes bandwidth utilization, lowers latency, increases privacy, and improves real-time processing. The future of edge computing in machine learning is being driven by breakthroughs in hardware, optimization techniques, and connectivity, despite obstacles like resource limits and data management. The combination of edge computing and machine learning will open up new possibilities and applications in a variety of fields as technology develops further

5. Common Applications of AI and ML

There are numerous uses for artificial intelligence (AI) and machine learning (ML) in a variety of sectors. The following are a few of the most popular uses:

8.1 Healthcare

- Imaging and diagnostics: AI models help analyze MRIs and X-rays to find diseases including cancer and neurological conditions.

- Predictive analytics: Machine learning algorithms forecast patient outcomes, facilitating tailored treatment regimens and preventive care.

- Drug Discovery: By finding promising chemicals and forecasting molecular behavior, artificial intelligence speeds up the drug discovery process.

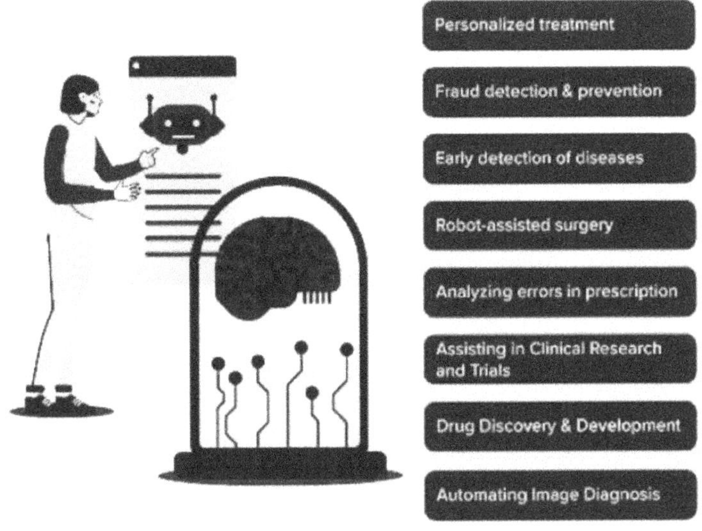

Figure.8.1 Healthcare for Applications Al and ML

8.2 Finance

- Fraud detection: To identify and stop fraudulent activity, machine learning algorithms examine transaction patterns.

- Risk management: AI evaluates portfolio management and credit risk, enhancing decision-making.

- Trading Algorithms: Using an analysis of market data, AI-driven trading algorithms maximize investing methods.

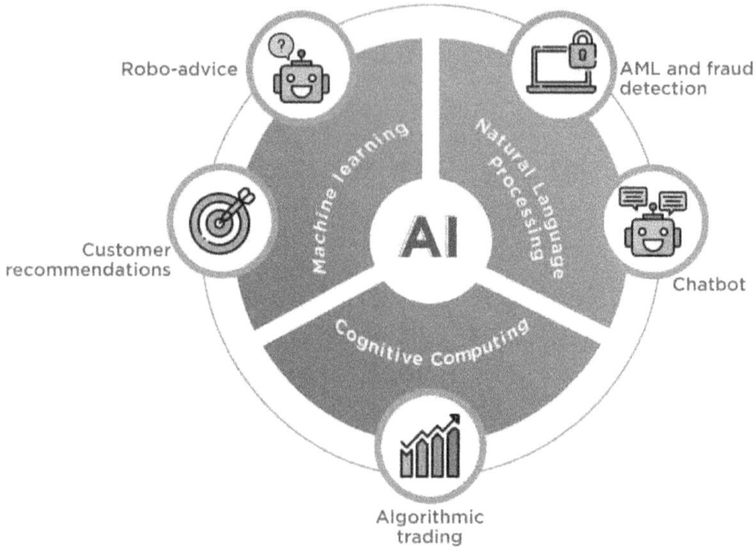

Figure.8.2 Finance for Applications Al and ML

8.3 Retail

- Customized Recommendations: AI makes product recommendations to users based on their past browsing and purchasing activity.

- Inventory management: To minimize overstock and stock outs, machine learning forecasts demand and optimizes inventory levels.

- Customer service is handled by catboats and virtual assistants, who also provide customer support.

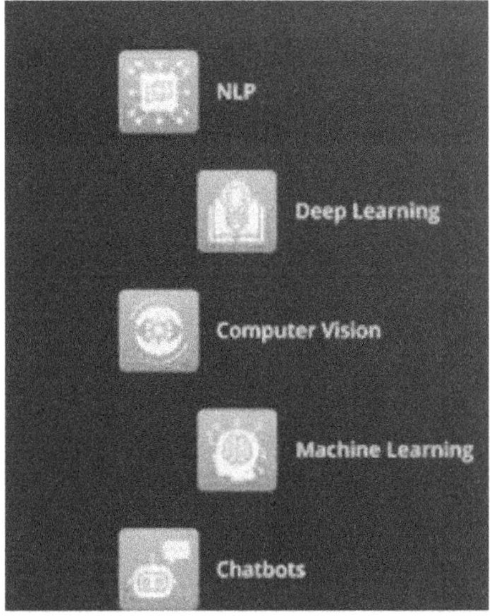

Figure.8.3 Retail for Applications Al and ML

8.4 Manufacturing

- AI-powered predictive maintenance lowers maintenance costs and downtime by anticipating equipment faults before they happen.

- Quality Control: To ensure high standards in industrial processes, ML models check products for flaws.

- Supply Chain Optimization: By predicting demand and overseeing logistics, artificial intelligence (AI) improves supply chain processes.

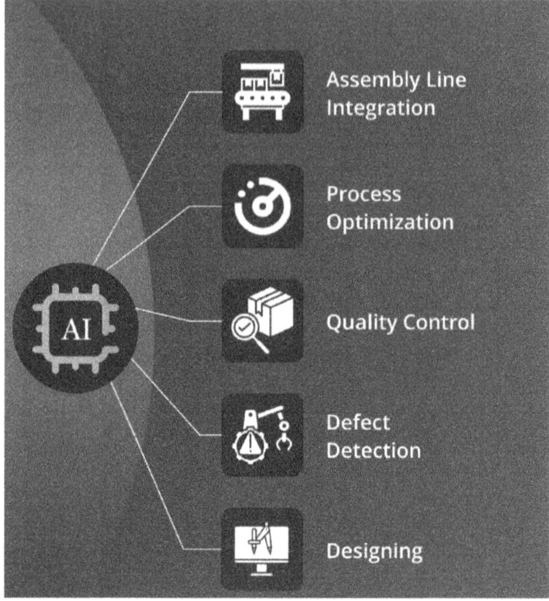

Figure.8.4 Manufacturing for Applications Al and ML

8.5 Automotive

- Autonomous Vehicles: Artificial intelligence (AI) uses sensor data processing to enable self-driving automobiles to navigate and make choices.

- AI improves safety functions like collision avoidance, adaptive cruise control, and lane departure warnings in driver assistance systems.

- Machine learning (ML) tracks the condition of vehicles and forecasts their maintenance requirements.

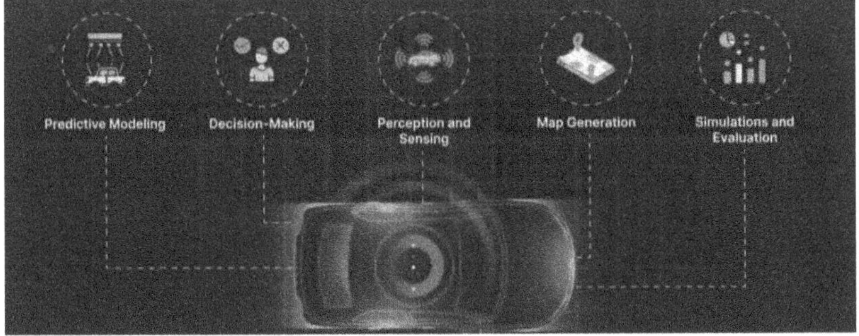

Figure.8.5 Automotive for Applications Al and ML

8.6 Marketing and Advertising

- Customer Segmentation: To create audiences for focused marketing initiatives, AI segments customers based on their data.

- Ad Optimization: To maximize return on investment, ML algorithms optimize ad placements and bidding tactics.

- Sentiment Analysis: AI examines data and social media to determine how customers feel about particular businesses and items.

Figure.8.6 Marketing and Advertising for Applications Al and ML

8.7 Telecommunications

- Network Optimization: By anticipating and addressing problems, AI maximizes the performance and dependability of networks.

- Customer service: Virtual assistants respond to questions from clients and solve issues.

- Churn Prediction: Machine learning models determine which clients are most likely to leave and recommend retention tactics.

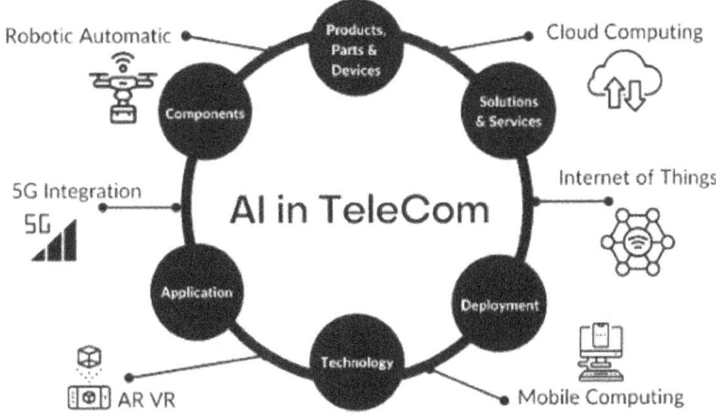

Figure.8.7 Telecommunications for Applications Al and ML

8.8 Education

AI-generated individualized learning programs are made in accordance with student performance and learning preferences.

Automated Grading: Machine learning provides prompt feedback by automatically grading assignments and tests.

Tutoring Systems: AI-driven tutoring systems provide students with on-demand help and support.

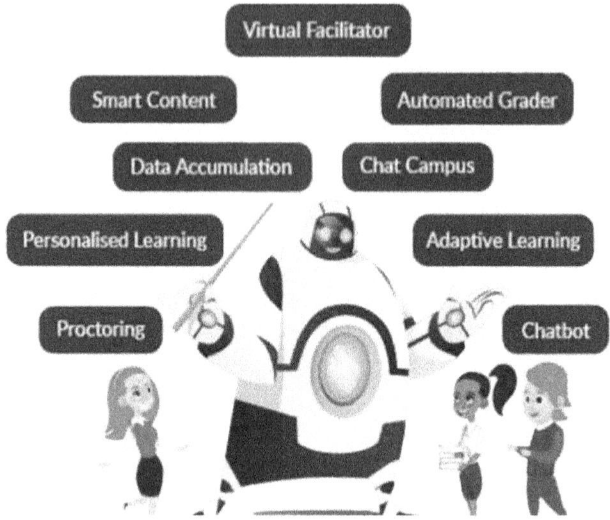

Figure.8.8 Education for Applications Al and ML

8.9 Energy

Smart Grids: Artificial intelligence (AI) efficiently balances supply and demand by optimizing energy distribution in smart grids.

Predictive Maintenance: ML keeps an eye on and forecasts the need for maintenance on energy-related infrastructure.

Energy Management: AI controls building energy usage to save expenses and increase efficiency.

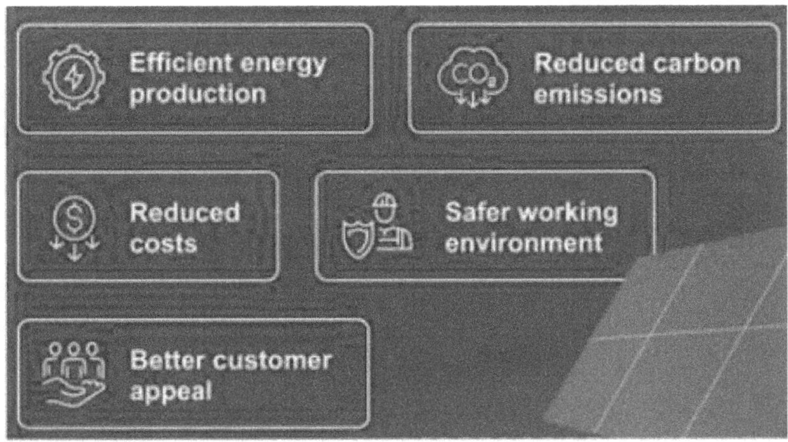

Figure.8.9 Energy for Applications Al and ML

8.10 Entertainment

Content Recommendation: AI uses user preferences to suggest TV shows, movies, music, and other types of content.

Content Creation: AI helps with scriptwriting, graphics, and even music production.

AI in gaming: By producing intelligent NPCs and flexible game environments, AI improves player experiences.

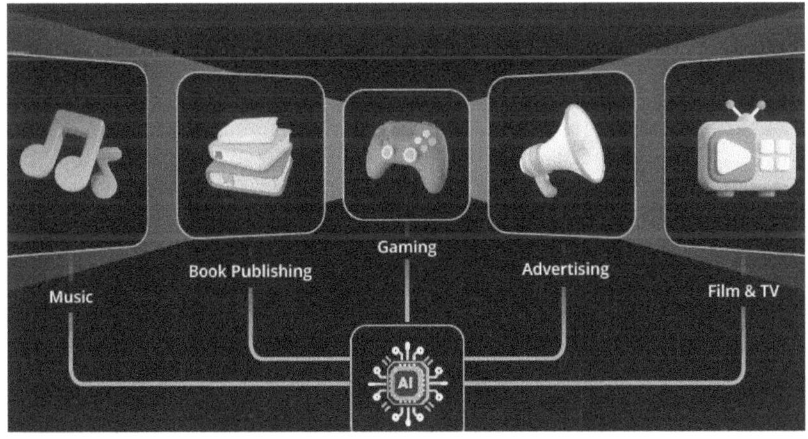

Figure.8.10 Entertainment for Applications Al and ML

8.11 Security

Artificial intelligence (AI) in surveillance scans video footage for unusual activity and improves security monitoring.

Threat Detection: Machine learning models identify potential attacks and cybersecurity threats.

Biometric Authentication: Artificial Intelligence drives biometric authentication technologies such as facial recognition.

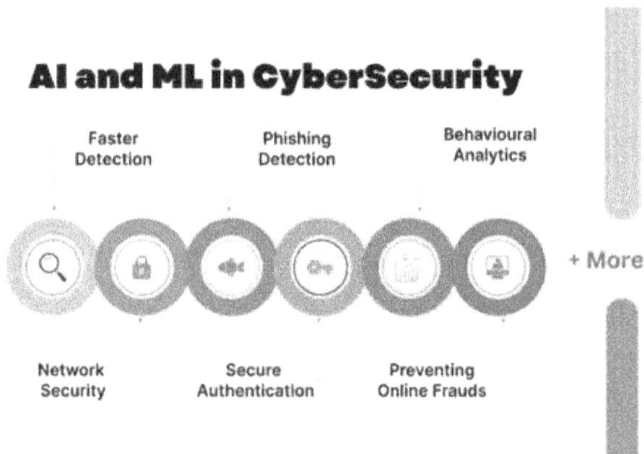

Figure.8.11 Security for Applications Al and ML

8.12 Logistics and Transportation

Route Optimization: AI plans delivery routes to maximize efficiency and minimize fuel use.

Supply Chain Management: To optimize the supply chain, machine learning forecasts demand and controls inventory levels.

AI fleet management keeps an eye on and oversees fleets of vehicles to ensure optimal upkeep and operational effectiveness.

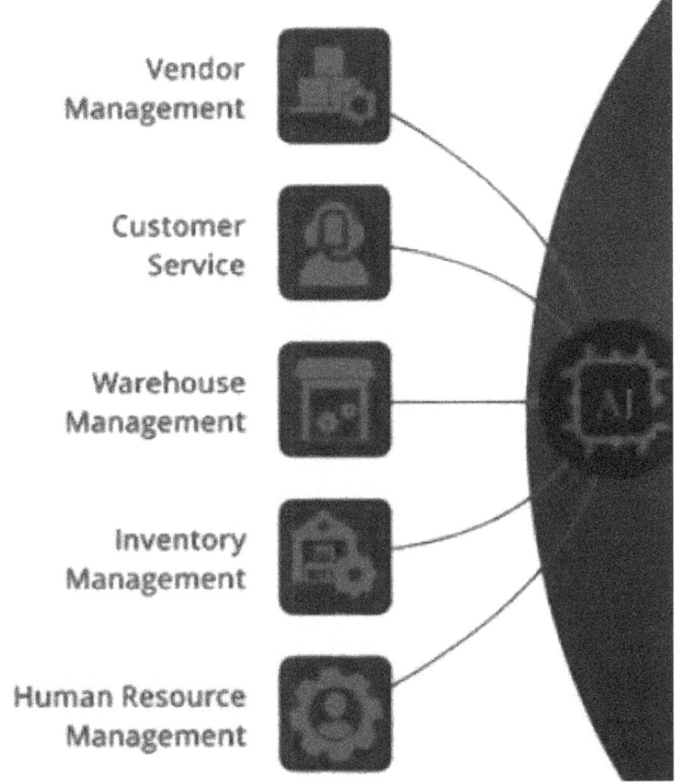

Figure.8.12 Logistics and Transportation for Applications Al and ML

www.ingramcontent.com/pod-product-compliance
Lightning Source LLC
Chambersburg PA
CBHW041314120726
48005CB00014B/1997